# FOOD AND COOKING OF
# SOUTH AFRICA

# FOOD AND COOKING OF
# SOUTH AFRICA

## FERGAL CONNOLLY
### PHOTOGRAPHY BY NICKI DOWEY

LORENZ BOOKS

# Contents

# INTRODUCTION

The food of South Africa is a unique fusion of cooking traditions from around the globe, which have coalesced into a balanced and harmonious cuisine. We shot the images for this book on location, buying fresh local ingredients and cooking the recipes on beaches of the Western Cape, in Dutch colonial kitchens, and on campfires and braais all over the the country. The recipes we've included are from the home kitchens of townships, inner cities, suburbs, vineyards and farms; each dish is individually delicious, but together they create a vibrant portrait of the home cooking of a remarkable nation.

*Fergal Connolly*

# A UNIQUE ENVIRONMENT

South Africa is blessed with bountiful natural resources and a climate and topography that has considerable variety. Its temperate zones are moderated by oceans on three sides, and the country is famous for its year-round sunshine, which results in such benign growing conditions that some crops can be harvested all year round.

The south-western side of the Cape enjoys warm dry summers and cool damp winters, while the eastern side is semi-tropical with plenty of rainfall throughout the year. Home to over 18,000 species of plants, of which over 80% occur nowhere else, the soil and climate conditions here mean that it is possible to produce almost any kind of food crop. From maize to tropical fruits, from butternut squash to the grapes grown in the beautiful vineyards of Stellenbosch, South Africa's farms are able to successfully grow an astonishing variety of ingredients.

The country's coastline stretches over 2,400km (1,500 miles) from the cool South Atlantic in the Western Cape to the warm tropical waters of the Indian Ocean. The Benguela current of the south-western coast creates a unique habitat, where diverse and abundant nutrients from the cold deep are carried to shallower waters, creating ideal conditions to support a rich marine life, both on and off shore.

Inland, South Africa's largest biome is its grasslands, which cover nearly a third of the country and are home to wild and farmed animals, including antelope, ostrich, fat-tailed sheep, goats and cattle; both European breeds and the native Nguni.

The country's second-largest biome is the great Karoo plateau, where rocky hills and mountains rise from sparsely populated scrubland. Although very dry, especially in the north-west towards the Kalahari desert, the Karoo is rich in shrubs and herbs – known as fynbos – which offer grazing for a special breed of sheep. North of the Vaal River the Highveld has higher rainfalls, and its altitude saves it from severe heat, while further north and to the east temperatures rise to extremes in the Bushveld region, famous for its wildlife. The deep interior sees the hottest temperatures, with Limpopo Province recording the highest. Buffelsfontein, in the Eastern Cape, is the coldest place in South Africa, and the majestic Drakensberg mountain range forms the country's eastern escarpment; home to ski resorts as well as icy, swift-flowing rivers and wide lakes where fish are plentiful.

With such diverse temperatures and geographical zones it is no wonder that the food produced in the country is plentiful and varied. This, added to the rich cooking traditions of indigenous peoples, colonists, Cape Malay and Indian workers, gives South Africa its wonderful rainbow cuisine.

## South Africa's culinary history

The cuisine of South Africa is a harmonious melting-pot of influences, from its indigenous peoples to the migrants who have arrived over the centuries. The expansion and evolution of its food and cooking traditions can be tracked by the journeys of the country's inhabitants and begins with San people who lived a nomadic existence in the Kalahari desert and along the coasts. The Dutch settlers who arrived in the 16th century were soon joined by Cape Malay slaves from Indonesia as well as other European pioneers from Britain and Germany. Boer voortrekkers gradually began to move into the interior of the country, while Portuguese traders travelled southwards from central Africa, and migrant workers arrived from all over India.

The history of South Africa's food can perhaps be divided into two eras, pre-colonial times – when the inhabitants were mainly nomadic hunter-gatherers – and the colonial era, which included the African, European, Malay and Indian influences.

## Pre-colonial South Africa

Information about this era comes mainly from archaeological findings, but the San people were the first inhabitants of South Africa, long before the arrival of the Bantu-speaking nations and thousands of years before the arrival of Europeans. It is thought that they were primarily nomadic hunter-gatherers, but adapted to herding domestic livestock in around 2200BC, moving south into the Highveld.

**The Klein Karoo has a harsh climate of extreme temperatures.**

Another San group, who became known as the Khoisan, moved their cattle into the lush Western Cape in the winter months, and then further north and east in the summer to take advantage of the seasonal rains. On the coast other San-derived people focused their food gathering on seafood: black mussels, ribbed mussels, limpets, whelks and abalone, prised from rocks and cooked over open fires.

These early settlers and nomadic herders had a varied diet of game, wild roots, berries, caterpillars, termites, locusts, wild honey and fish, unchanged for centuries and still being harvested and cooked in the same way when the first Europeans arrived. Plentiful game was driven into traps, while grasslands were adapted to corral the game into hunting areas, that were later developed into pasture for farmed cattle. Trade links with other tribes in the region were formed, and metals such as iron and copper were exchanged for sheep and cattle.

Some time between 300BC and 500BC Bantu-speaking nations, including the Nguni and Sotho, began arriving in the South African region. Although they had a completely different language system and a more advanced Iron Age culture it would seem that they co-existed with the original San inhabitants, until the arrival of European colonists who within two centuries almost completely destroyed the nomadic hunter-gatherers, pushing them into the Kalahari Desert of Namibia where they remained in relative isolation.

Elements of early foods still remain in the modern South African diet. The first cooked grain was sorghum, still eaten today, but often replaced by maize. A typical meal in a South

African Bantu-speaking home will still include 'pap', a stiff, fluffy porridge of sorghum or maize meal, served with a flavourful meat gravy. Fermented milk, or amasi, is also still made and enjoyed in the same way as it always has been. Beef was considered the most important and high status meal, cooked on an open fire, an influence on the diet that is reflected today in the universal national love of the braai.

## Dutch settlers

A fearsome European force both at sea and on land in the 16th century, Holland has had arguably one of the greatest political and cultural influences on South African society. The Dutch East India Trading Company (Vereenigde Oostindische Compagnie, or VOC) was keen to establish an outpost for its ships making their way to and from the spice-laden lands of the East Indies. Transporting goods was difficult by land as it meant having to use Arab middlemen to ensure passage through the slow and treacherous trade route of the Silk Road. In order to transport cargo safely and securely by sea, Commander Jan Van Riebeeck was dispatched to the Western Cape by the Lords Seventeen of the VOC with orders to establish a protected harbour that could refresh, repair and resupply ships and crews.

During the 15th century British and Portuguese ships had regularly landed in the Cape to trade cattle and metal with the local San people without making any real impact on the region. On the 6th April 1652, however, Jan Van Riebeeck arrived into Table Bay, a natural harbour along the top of the Cape Peninsula, and within just two weeks had laid out and established a market garden to produce fruit and vegetables. This plantation was later known as Company Gardens, and it is still in existence today in the centre of Cape Town.

It is recorded that the first meal the early Dutch settlers ate, that was sourced from the land they were making their home, consisted of foraged sorrel plants and wild mustard leaves along with freshly caught fish. Foods that were planted included pumpkin, cucumber, sweet potato, apples, pears, quinces and watermelon, and these early trial plantings were to have a lasting impact on the national cuisine. Passing ships also left some of their cargo with the locals, including spices like pepper, coriander, nutmeg and allspice, all of which were very much at the forefront of what was to become the South African palate.

Initial contact with local tribes was generally confused and mistrustful. The settlers found it difficult to breed cattle and sheep and felt that in their attempts to trade animals with local herdsmen they only got the poorest of the herd, so penguins, seals and seagulls were often served at the dinner table. Sourcing seafood was much more successful, and the Dutch were lucky enough to come across the rock lobster or crayfish of the Western Cape, known locally today as kreef.

**Table Bay and the growing settlement of Cape Town, 1820.**

**Tsaarsbank, in the West Coast National Park.**

**St Augustine Anglican Church in Paternoster, built in 1888.**

This early European settlement was not just inhabited by the Dutch but sometimes by the passengers of their ships, including immigrants from Europe, as well as Chinese convicts, prisoners from Java and slaves from Mozambique who were all used as labour in the gardens, giving the Cape an almost cosmopolitan feel. As the community grew, tensions gradually increased between the New World arrivals and their hosts and Van Riebeeck firstly erected a fence of (poisonous) wild almond trees to ward off the threat of his crops being stolen and to mark their territory, and then a fort.

Van Riebeeck left the Cape in 1662, but in the ten years under his command the outpost had progressed rapidly. In the Company Gardens and its surrounds he had managed to plant over 160 citrus trees and 70 other fruit trees, and in addition to the thriving vegetable garden had also laid out a herb and medicinal garden, and had planted rose and oak trees. By 1659 he had also started a fledgling wine and brandy distilling industry to refresh the throngs of thirsty locals, and sailors who were passing through. To source sufficient labour to achieve this Van Riebeeck had also overseen the procurement of a considerable number of slaves, convicts and political prisoners.

There were, however, difficulties in producing carbohydrates to accompany the main meal. Van Riebeeck repeatedly tried to cultivate rice, a favourite starch of the Dutch as well as a staple in the diet of the slaves and convicts. All attempts at growing it failed, however, and it had to be imported on most ships that entered the Cape.

Van Riebeeck needed overseers and managers as well as labourers in his venture, and he succeeded in persuading the VOC to release some of their staff from their contracts in order to take responsibility for plots of land. These new farms would grow produce for the increasing demand of the community, and ships that stopped for supplies. The early farmers were known as Free Burghers and their smallholdings created original recipes, and adapted older ones, to the ingredients.

The Dutch Reform Church was brought to the Cape from Holland by the first Dutch settlers, and initially was part of the Dutch East India Trading Company. It formed a pioneering and town-planning role in the Great Trek, where when a church was founded and secured in a new settlement it was then allowed to grant plots of land to settlers.

By the first half of the 1700s the subsistence farmer descendants of these Free Burghers, and other Dutch settlers, were starting to chafe against the autocratic rule of the VOC, which they saw as corrupted, and they began to trek northwards and eastwards into the interior to find better pastures. These intrepid families were the first Trek Boers, and travelling with their herds they lived a relatively nomadic life. By the end of the 18th century there were some settlements on the wider plains where initially they were given some land by the VOC, but still they moved inland, meeting with little resistance as they dispossessed the Khoisan tribes of their herds, territories and in some cases their lives. Constantly in search of new land the Trek Boers frequently reloaded their ox wagons to pursue greener pastures, and so established the national character of the Africaan Boers, and paved the way for the Great Trek.

## British rule

During the Napoleonic Wars in Europe, the Cape colony was annexed by the British, and in 1815 it became their property. Like the Dutch before them, Britain's main interest in the settlement was its importance as a strategically located port. When they arrived in the Cape they found a troubled society that consisted of 25,000 slaves, 20,000 white colonials, 15,000 Khoisan and 1,000 freed black slaves, while the countryside outside was populated by isolated black and white pastoralists. To stabilize this fragmented society the British persuaded 5,000 middle-class intrepid citizens to emigrate from the UK to South Africa and take possession of tracts of land lying between the feuding Boer and African communities. Eventually this new British contingent created its own division, fracturing the previously united white element into two, and a pattern soon emerged of English-speakers occupying the towns and urban areas – dominating politics, trade and finance – while the largely uneducated Boers were relegated to their farms. This cultural divide was made even more acute when the British abolished slavery in 1833, a move that the Boers regarded as against a natural order ordained by God.

## Voortrekkers

From about 1838 groups of Dutch-speaking Afrikaans moved from town to town towards the north of the country. Bitterly opposed to many aspects of British rule they set off with their ox wagons in huge numbers to search for new pastures where they could establish their own laws and customs. This movement to areas outside the reach of the British authorities

Boerewors.

Traditional houses of the Drakensberg region.

Bunny chow.

led to the foundation of the Boer states of Natal Republic and the Orange Free State. This successful pioneering venture was later to be known as the Great Trek, and its significance on the cuisine, as well as the psyche of the nation, cannot be underestimated. As they trekked in their wagons across the harshest of terrain the Boers preserved their meat by air-drying it. They cooked everything, from soups and stews to bread, pies and cookies on the campfire, often using the traditional huge cast-iron pots called potjies, or Dutch ovens.

## German bread-making

As the outpost at Cape Colony was being established there were many arrivals and departures, and at one point there were more Germans at the Cape than Dutch. They were mostly single men, however, and they were eventually integrated through marriage into the Dutch population.

During the 19th century the colonial authorities issued a special dispensation, which allowed Germans to emigrate to the Cape, and they arrived in huge numbers, this time as whole families, bringing with them baking and brewing skills, of which there is still some evidence today. German bakeries in Cape Town and Stellenbosch still make dark rye wild yeast breads in traditional wood-fired ovens, while the making of sausages, in particular boerewors, has also left its mark.

## French Huguenot wines

The Huguenots were French Protestant refugees who arrived in South Africa around 1688, fleeing religious persecution from the Catholic Church. Although small in numbers (about 200) they quickly dispersed themselves into the Western Cape region. The language was lost after the first generation, as emotional links with France had diminished because of their exiled status, but using their vast knowledge of viticulture, they became involved in South Africa's fledgling wine-making industry. This had been set up by the Dutch, but with poor results, and The Dutch East India Company granted land to the French refugees in Franschhoek (French corner). It is this area that produces some of the most noted South African wines today.

The French settlers were also great preservers, bottling fruit and making jams and confiture, skills which were eagerly adopted by the Dutch and are still in evidence today. The French also influenced menu courses at mealtimes, such as the tradition of serving soup before the main course.

## Cape Malay spices

The first slaves imported by the Dutch were from Java – modern-day Indonesia – and were largely speakers of the Malayu language, hence their adopted name of Cape Malays. The Javanese community was later added to by slaves from various other Southeast Asian regions, and also from India.

The Cape Malays have had a very important influence on the national palate, as the VOC bought skilled carpenters, fishermen, musicians, tailors and excellent cooks who understood how to balance flavours, whether that was spices with cooling citrus sambals or sweet chutneys to enhance the rich roasted game. Soon after their arrival in the Cape dishes such as bobotie, atjar, and blatjang worked their way onto the Cape table. Quince chutney is an excellent example of how the Malay cooks took a new-found ingredient – quince – and combined it with the their own cooking traditions to make a brand-new accompaniment that would be a South African favourite to the present day.

On the slopes of Signal Hill in Cape Town lies the Bo-Kaap. This unique area has retained the architecture, food and culture of the Cape Malays. The pastel-coloured houses are still inhabited by descendants of the original people who arrived from the east, bringing a vibrant cuisine to their new homeland, and among them are small shops and restaurants that still sell and serve the traditional cuisine.

## Portuguese traders

Portugal's empire once spanned a huge area, from the imposing Grand Banks of the eastern coast of the United States, where they encountered huge codfish that they preserved as salt-cod or bacalau, to the Southern Atlantic coast of Brazil, and from the Cape Verde Islands to the spice-laden East Indies of Goa, Cochin and Galle.

The Portuguese initially navigated around the Cape of Good Hope in 1486, where they landed only briefly to trade livestock before continuing east on the 'trade winds' that they had discovered would make a sea-route from Europe to the East Indies possible. Although laying claim to this outpost, instead of populating, inhabiting and colonizing it like the Dutch, they simply dropped crosses marked with the Portuguese coat of arms, before pressing further on towards the Indian coast in search of spices and other treasures. It wasn't until the 20th century that the Portuguese began to travel back into

Curry leaves.

A potjie on a campfire.

A store selling samoosas and sosaties, Imizamo Yetho Township.

South Africa after their two colonies of Mozambique and Angola had gained independence.

Portuguese food and culture was quickly absorbed into mainstream South African cooking, with dishes like grilled sardines and the prego roll steak sandwich, as well as peri-peri dishes made with the tiny fiery chillies of the same name found in Mozambique and Angola, becoming firm favourites on the menus of cafes and restaurants of South Africa. Possibly the most well-known culinary alliance between South Africa and Portugal came in 1987, when a restaurant called Nando's was opened in Rosettenville on the eastern side of Johannesburg. It served peri-peri spiced grilled chicken to migrant Portuguese workers, and has expanded to become an international chain.

## Indian plantation workers

The majority of Indian people arriving in South Africa came in two migration waves. The first group of around 150,000 came between 1860 and 1911 as 'indentured' travellers or servants, which meant they had to work for five years for their initial employer before looking for another position. Most were hard-working Hindus who came to the Natal colony, which at the time was under British control, from the south and north-east of India, to work on the sugar plantations. The South African sugar cane industry was established at the end of the 1840s when sugar was planted in trials in semi-tropical Natal. This was mostly grown for exporting back to Britain, which had developed an insatiable appetite for all things sweet. The trial also included experimental planting of coffee, arrowroot, cotton and tobacco. Sugar proved to be the most successful crop in a climate that is semi-tropical, has plenty of sunshine and good amounts of rainfall, and it was widely adopted.

The other group of Indian immigrants were known as 'passenger Indians' (because they paid their own way to South Africa). They came mostly from the west coast of India and were often traders and merchants. Some were also Christian teachers and priests.

The impact of Indian cuisine has been particularly influential along the Natal coastline, and the most famous dish from this region is the hugely popular bunny chow. This dish was created by Indians on the sugar plantations in the 19th century, and involves hollowing out half a small government-produced loaf of bread, and filling it with a carefully balanced spiced curry containing pulses and vegetables or mutton. The hollowed-out bread is placed on top like a little hat to absorb the delicious juicy curry, and it is then wrapped in newspaper to be taken to the fields to be eaten at midday, without cutlery, as is the Indian way.

Another great legacy of the Indian migrants can be found in the downtown area of Durban known as the Victoria Street Market. Built in 1910 the market pays homage to the pink palaces of the Maharajah and still sells ground spices, meat, fish and fruit and vegetables as well as traditional crafts and jewellery. The cafes in the market also serve bunny chow to hungry patrons.

## The melting pot of South Africa

By the mid-18th century the ethnic cooking traditions of South Africa had begun to merge. The predominant Dutch and Malay cultures had shared the secrets of their respective dishes and the result of this was a national cuisine with an established South African palate. These firm links to the past are being pushed forwards through the 21st century with a thriving food scene in Cape Town that boasts distinguished and internationally-renowned restaurants. Artisan producers are also at the forefront of the new food renaissance with producers re-discovering traditional cheese-making, flour-milling, brewing, and chocolate-making skills.

Styles of cookery have also been retained. Braais are always a great South African social event, across all class and ethnic divides. Men gathering around a fire, talking about rugby, football or cricket while the smell of smoky meat or seafood fills the air is practically a national pastime. There is even a National Braai Day on 24 September each year, although people hardly need any encouragement.

Slow cooking also has its place, and there has been a resurgence in the use of potjies for long, slow-cooked stews and curries. Originally these big, cast-iron pots were used by the Voortrekkers as they migrated across the interior of the country, and their continued use is another historical and social link across the generations.

The recipes in this book celebrate South Africa's cultural inheritance, offering authentic dishes that reflect a vibrant and ever-changing society. We hope our love for this unique country, with its fabulous cuisine, will inspire you to explore the delights of its food and cooking.

# INGREDIENTS

## *Meat and game*

**Biltong.**

Throughout its history, from the earliest times to the present day, the inhabitants of South Africa have put meat at the centre of a meal, especially beef and game.

### ANTELOPE

There are many different types of African antelope that roam the veld and open pastures of western and central South Africa. The two most common are the springbok and kudu, which both make excellent biltong but are also good in a casserole or stew. The animals' diet of fresh grasses, shrubs and herbs impart the flesh with wonderful flavour.

### CROCODILE

Most of the crocodile meat sold in South Africa is the Nile crocodile species. It is bred commercially for its skin as well as its flesh, but is considered a wild meat. Usually only the tail is consumed. The meat holds up to strong flavours and can be simply seared on a braai and served with spicy chillies and tropical fruits.

### BEEF

In the lush green fields of the KwaZulu-Natal midlands there is a whole host of dairy and beef farms, and beef is probably the most popular meat in the country for all kinds of dishes. Indigenous Nguni cattle, identified by their long necks and multi-coloured hides, are a hardy breed that thrive well in the South African grasslands, although their meat to carcass ratio is inferior to European breeds.

### BILTONG

A South African way of preserving meat from the days before refrigeration, air-dried beef or game was a more convenient way of carrying meat on the move. Lobes of fresh meat are flavoured with salt, spices and malt vinegar and then hung to dry for a number of days. The Voortrekkers would serve thin slices of biltong with rendered fat spread on baked pot bread, accompanied by pickled vegetables.

### BOEREWORS

Meaning 'farmer sausage' this traditional South African sausage of Dutch origin consists of coarsely chopped or ground meat, usually beef or pork, spiked with pepper, coriander seeds, nutmeg and allspice.

### KAROO LAMB AND MUTTON

Although mostly barren and semi-arid the Karoo and Klein Karoo regions are full of grazing animals. Genuine Karoo certification means that the animals are fed exclusively on the uncultivated scrubby bushes and grass known as the karoobossie, which gives a herbaceous-like flavour to the flesh. The sheep are identifiable by their fat tails and woolly coats, and although the climate can be punishingly hot in summer these hardy animals thrive, and produce outstanding, flavourful meat.

### OSTRICH

In the Klein Karoo region, and particularly around Oudtshroon, ostrich are farmed commercially both for their feathers and meat. Ostrich has some of the characteristics of poultry but is actually a red meat, and its low fat content makes it a great healthy protein choice. Fillet is excellent for a braai; the neck lends itself to slower, cooked dishes like potjies; and ostrich burger is also commonplace on many menus across the country.

### MOPANE OR MOPANI WORMS

Perhaps more popular in neighbouring Botswana and Zimbabwe, these worms have been a source of protein for generations. They are traditionally eaten in the more rural parts of the country and are usually dried then roasted over a fire, and served with ground peanuts and mealie pap.

**Nguni cattle.**

**Kudu.**

**Karoo lamb.**

**Mopane worms.**

# Fish and shellfish

With such rich seas and large inland waters, fish and shellfish are plentiful in South Africa and are enjoyed when grilled on the braai. Cape Town in particular is becoming internationally famous for its outstanding seafood restaurants.

### BOKKOMS
A West Coast speciality, bokkoms, or harders – also known as Bombay duck by English settlers – are preserved fillets of Southern Ocean mullet. Carried on treks as a good source of protein, they are prepared by firstly salting them and then hanging them in bunches outside in the strong south-westerly breeze of the Western Cape for about 10 days. They can be used to garnish a soup or pep up a salad.

### CAPE SALMON
This species of salmon, also known locally as geelback (yellow mouth), has a similar look to the North Atlantic salmon species but its flesh is white and slightly opaque. Depleted stocks mean that this much-loved migratory fish has become less common in fish markets. It is mostly caught by line, or rod and reel, along the Natal coast.

### CRAYFISH
Also known to the locals as kreef, this small-sized spiny lobster is a Western Cape speciality. It is caught in abundance at the West Coast town of Paternoster, where local fishermen can be seen in brightly coloured boats called bakkies. The legality of fishing for these much-sought shellfish is the subject of much debate as stocks deteriorate and poaching increases.

### EASTERN CAPE OYSTERS
Oysters are in great demand throughout the country, both wild and cultivated, and along the KwaZulu-Natal coast they are harvested by hand amongst the rocky reefs.

### KINGKLIP
Considered a fine, firm, table fish, the kingklip's liver is considered a real delicacy. This fish can reach a whopping 180cm/6ft in length, and can withstand the slow cooking of a potjie and the warm spices of the Cape Malay cuisine.

### GIANT YELLOWTAIL
These big fish live in the cold Atlantic waters off the Cape. During the annual sardine run, they migrate towards the east coast of southern Africa to feast on the sardines.

### PERLEMOEN
This sea snail is part of the abalone family. Considered to be a rare delicacy, abalone is now illegal to fish for but there are still many aquaculture farms producing this slow-growing shellfish. It is usually sold pre-cooked in cans and is very expensive.

### SNOEK
A local fish found close to the coast along the cool waters of the Western Cape, snoek is sometimes lightly smoked. It has firm white flesh that holds flavour well and is ideal cooked over a braai or made into boboties.

### TROUT
Both brown and rainbow trout were introduced by Scottish settlers to the rivers and lakes of the KwaZulu-Natal and the Drakensberg in the 1890s. Mostly farmed today, there are still some wild stocks available to the keen fly angler in the waters of this region.

# Vegetables and fruit

The varied climate and geography of South Africa means that a wide variety of crops can be grown all round the farming year, and the local markets of the country are full of all kinds of fruit and vegetables.

### CORN OR MEALIES
A vital staple crop in South Africa, maize replaced sorghum as the most popular grain, and it is now the main carbohydrate of the region. It is generally accepted that the Portuguese brought corn or maize to Africa from their colonies in the Americas, and it is now grown mainly in the Free State and the Natal Midlands. Grilled mealie cobs are often found at refreshment stops along the roadside, while ground maize, known as mealie meal in South Africa, is used in many recipes.

### PAP
Maize pap is made from mealie meal. It is often eaten as porridge in the morning with milk and honey, or as a starch to accompany juicy meats, or with a rich tomato and onion sauce. Pap is also an accompaniment to the fiery relish known as chakalaka. When served dry and crumbly it is also known as phutupap.

Crayfish.

Perlemoen.

Bokkoms.

Giant yellowtail.

### MEALIE PAP

Similar to polenta, mealie pap can be soft or dry; this recipe makes a fairly stiff mixture, which serves two.

170g/6oz/1 cup mealie meal, sorghum or cornmeal
750ml/1¼ pints/3 cups water
salt, to taste
25g/1oz/2 tbsp butter

**1** Place the water in a heavy pan, add a good pinch of salt and bring to the boil. Slowly pour in the mealie meal, stirring so that no lumps form. Cook for 3–4 minutes, stirring constantly until the mixture thickens and forms a fairly solid texture, rather like mashed potato. Add more water if you want a looser consistency.

**2** Turn the heat down to as low as possible, add small knobs of butter on the top, cover with a lid and cook for 15–20 minutes. The bottom of the pap should develop a golden crust, which is delicious, but if it burns even slightly it will be bitter.

**3** Serve the pap hot, with stew or soup, or chakalaka. Or add sugar and serve with warm milk for breakfast.

Samp.

### SAMP

This is dried, coarsely chopped corn that has an almost bean-like texture when cooked. In African communities samp is often served with beans and peanuts, whereas the Dutch call it stampmielies and serve it with meat dishes or used as a stuffing for poultry.

### SORGHUM

A great staple in the drier parts of the country, and initially a wild grain, sorghum is similar to millet. It is mostly used to make porridge, or pap, but bread can also be made from ground sorghum. In some parts of the country sorghum is also fermented and made into beer.

### AVOCADO

The first avocado orchard in South Africa was planted in 1920 in the Transvaal region, and the industry has thrived since then as they are now available virtually the whole year round. Often the main ingredients of salads and sambals, avocados are also enjoyed with steak and burgers.

### BUTTERNUT SQUASH

This long-lasting golden-fleshed squash is so plentiful throughout the country that farm stalls sell them in sacks of 15 or so. A favourite ingredient in side dishes and soups, they are typically lightly spiced.

### SWEET POTATOES

South Africans love sweet potatoes, and usually they are served with succulent grilled meats from the braai. Baked with sweet honey, they can be cooked on the hot coals of a campfire and can be seen on the menus of many fine restaurants throughout the country. They thrive in the warm sunny climate of South Africa, and the major production areas are Limpopo, Mpumalanga, Natal and the Western Cape.

### UINTJIES

Meaning 'small onion' in Dutch, uintjies is a collective name for a group of plants with edible roots or bulbs, which are unique to South Africa. They were eaten by the San long before the Dutch arrived and tried to identify each variety with names like baboon, goat, thick-skinned, mountain and bushman uintjies. They are still gathered and eaten in the Kalahari, where they are roasted in hot ash or boiled in milk.

### WATERBLOMMETJIES

These small white-flowered water lilies are a winter and early spring phenomena that grow on the top of the wetlands and waterways of the Western Cape, and whose stems and flowers can be cooked and eaten. Waterblommetjies are washed scrupulously in salted water before cooking to remove sand, grit and bugs. Also available canned, they feature in the Cape classic waterblommetjies bredie, or stew.

### APRICOTS

Originally planted by the early VOC settlers in the Western Cape, today South Africa is one of the top growers of apricots in the world. The fruit is enjoyed fresh but is also bottled and made into preserves. Dense and delicious, apricot jam seems to feature in almost all Dutch colonial baking recipes in one way or another.

### PLUMS

Growers in South Africa's Western and Eastern Cape cultivate a wide range of delicious red, purple and yellow plums, which are exported widely and are famous for their sweetness.

Apricots.

Plums.

## CAPE GRAPES

The warmth of the sun and low humidity means that the Western Cape is an ideal place for producing sweet, juicy, seedless grapes, and it is said that vines were a great success when first planted at Van Riebeeck's Company Gardens. Raisins are believed to have first been exported from South Africa as early as 1745, and they are used in some of South Africa's favourite dishes including bobotie, yellow rice, and blatjang. Much of the raisin production industry is centred along the Orange River, an area that also produces excellent wines.

## FIGS

Traditionally the first crop of figs were removed from the tree while still 'green' – fully developed but firm and unripe. This allowed them to be pickled in sugar, syrup and spices and kept in the larder for later in the year. When the second crop arrived they were allowed to ripen on the tree and were eaten fresh, or dried. There are hundreds of types of figs grown in South Africa, and most of them thrive in the warm climate and soil of the Western Cape.

## LIMES

Very popular in South Africa for use in cooking and in drinks, limes and other citrus fruits grow well in many areas.

## MANGO

There is a long history of mango production in South Africa, and the fruit is grown over a wide area, concentrated in the Northern Province. Enjoyed ripe for desserts or in fresh sambals during December, the fruit is also heavily picked when green to make into mango atjar, the South African version of mango chutney.

## PEARS/APPLES

These orchard fruits can be found growing all over the Western Cape under heavy irrigation. The warm climate ensures that the fruit is sharp, crisp and sweet.

## PRICKLY PEARS

The fruit of the cactus, prickly pears can be seen growing wild throughout the dry semi-arid Karoo region, and are ready to eat when they turn pale pink. They are prepared by carefully peeling off the spiny skin, and can be eaten fresh or used to make jams and jellies.

## PEACHES

South Africa's peaches are a more recent addition to the country's fruit farms, and the celebrated yellow cling peaches are a speciality of the Klein Karoo region. These yellow-skinned peaches are surrounded by a thick fuzzy down that clings to the peach, making them tricky to peel, and are mostly sold in cans.

## PINEAPPLE

Because of the sub-tropical climate of the eastern coast, pineapples can be grown with little difficulty; the cool rains brought by the sea give the fruits natural irrigation. Simple to cook on the braai, slices of grilled pineapple go very well with barbecued fish or meat.

## QUINCE

First cultivated by Van Riebeeck, quince was one of the first successful fruits grown in the Company Gardens, and they are now grown throughout the country, especially in the Western Cape. Embraced by new settlers, quince jam is a firm favourite of the Cape Boer table, while quince sambal is a popular Malay accompaniment to a hot curry.

## SOUR FIGS

Native to South Africa, and also known as ice plant or Hottentot fig, these are dried and sold in huge sacks at market. They can also be eaten fresh. The flower of the sour fig is fiery red with a green base, and the fruit make wonderfully tart jam or konfyt.

## SUGAR CANE

Huge plantations of sugar cane make a significant contribution to South Africa's economy, and have been situated across the provinces of KwaZulu-Natal and Mpumalanga for over 150 years, since the first plants arrived from Mauritius. This was to have a big cultural effect on the region, as it heralded the arrival of migrant Indian workers.

# *Dairy products*

South African's love of milk-based products is another link between its north European influences and the ancient African tradition of nurturing herds of dairy cattle. Milk and cream are more often long-life than pasturized and cheeses tend to be quite mild. Cottage cheese, yogurt and fermented milk products like amasi are also produced commercially.

## AMASI

The Xhosa believe that amasi – fermented milk that tastes a bit like cottage cheese – makes a man strong, healthy and desirable. Nelson Mandela has told of how he was forced to leave his hiding place, a white comrade's apartment, when he overheard two Zulu workers outside comment how strange it was to see a pot of milk left outside to ferment, because whites seldom drank amasi. Since then, however, amasi has grown in popularity across ethnic divides, and is now sold commercially.

**Green figs.**

**Grapes.**

**Sour figs.**

**Amasi.**

Ostrich egg.

Rooibos tea.

Chakalaka.

### CHEESE

South African cheeses until recently tended to be mild, mass-produced copies of Dutch Gouda and English Cheddar. Today there is a new wave of artisan producers, from the Natal Midlands to Gauteng province and over to the Western Cape, making cheeses that are of excellent quality using the milk from European-style cattle like Ayrshires and Jerseys. Goat's cheeses are also being made with great success. Goats adapt well to the cold temperatures of the Drakensberg winter, as well as to extreme heat in the summer. Milch goats are commonly herded in South Africa; their milk is rich in nutrients and they adapt well to harsh terrains.

### OSTRICH EGGS

Rearing ostriches in South Africa has suffered from various setbacks, but Oudtshroon in the Klein Karoo now has well-established farms, which are a good place to see ostriches up close. The largest ostrich eggs will usually weigh about 1.5kg/3lb 3oz and are the equivalent of 24 hen's eggs. The flavour is similar to a hen's but the texture is slightly different, and they are usually made into omelettes or frittatas for large numbers of people.

## Condiments and tea

There are now many famous South African table condiments sold throughout the world. One of the more famous brands is Mrs Ball's Chutney, which symbolizes the great melting pot of South African cuisines and culture with its Hindi name, Malay spices and home grown fruit, mixed with the South African love of preserving, and appreciation of a balance in sweetness and spice. Other favourite homemade preserves include blatjang, originally imported from Indonesia but tempered and sweetened to suit the developing South African palate. Today blatjang is the pride of the Cape Malays. Other condiments include fresh and piquant sambals, often made to accompany a hot and spicy Malay curry.

### CHAKALAKA

Rooted in the townships of South Africa, chakalaka is a simple, spicy dish of onions, tomatoes and beans that is often served with braai dishes. It also makes a quick and easy accompaniment to mealie pap.

### SPICES

Fresh chillies and dried spices were introduced to South Africa by the Cape Malays, and are an important part of the nation's cuisine. Various dry spice mixtures are sold at markets in huge bowls or tubs. Some blends, like masala mix, are standard throughout the country, others are peculiar to a particular region or vendor and are given names like Chicken Lickin, or Terminator.

### WORCESTERSHIRE SAUCE

Introduced by the British settlers this is used as one of the flavourings in the traditional version of biltong.

### OLIVE OIL

Although a fledgling industry in South Africa there are many small producers of fine quality olive oil in the Western Cape. The relatively cool winters with little frost and the hot summers, aligned with the stony, well-aerated soil, is ideal for the cultivation of olives and olive oil.

### RUSKS

Originally adapted from the Dutch recipe for twice-baked biscuits, these long-lasting, hard-baked biscuits were carried by the Boers on their treks across the interior. Today the humble rusk has seen something of a renaissance in South African cooking. They are often served on bush camps and in safari lodges on early morning game drives, when they are dunked into coffee or hot chocolate.

### ROOIBOS TEA

This is a much-loved South African drink made from the rooibos plant, which is a member of the fynbos that grows in the Cape floral kingdom. The plant grows naturally only in the Cederberg Mountains of the Western Cape, a unique region with climatic and geological elements that combine to provide ideal growing conditions for the plants. The tea is low in tannin, caffeine-free and is widely enjoyed. It is also used in cooking as a marinade for sosaties, and in salad dressings.

### HONEYBUSH TEA

Similar to rooibos in that it is indigenous to South Africa, honeybush is also low in tannins and has no caffeine, making it a refreshing all-day drink. It is grown principally in the Eastern Cape. It is also said to protect against diabetes. The leaves are best brewed in hot water and drunk without milk.

### CHAKALAKA

This famous South African condiment is made commercially, but is very simple to make at home. It doesn't always contain beans, if you wish to have more of a sauce and less of a stew, leave them out.

**1** Heat 30ml/2 tbsp oil in a heavy pan and add 2 onions, chopped, 2 (bell) peppers, chopped, 2 red chillies, seeded and chopped, and 2 crushed cloves of garlic. Fry gently, stirring, for 5–8 minutes, until the onions are cooked and transparent.

**2** Add 10ml/1 tsp curry powder and 3 chopped tomatoes and bring to the boil, then reduce the heat and simmer for about 5 minutes. Stir in a can of baked beans in tomato sauce, heat through, adding salt and pepper to taste, and serve hot or cold.

# WATER AND WINE

The conundrum of finding water is always a matter of concern in South Africa, while in contrast the well-watered and productive vineyards of the Western Cape produce a liquid that is exported and enjoyed all over the world.

## WATER

Section 27 of the bill of rights of the constitution of South Africa states that everyone must have access to sufficient water and food. Given the shortage of water in some parts of the country this obligation continues to challenge politicians and administrators, and is still unfulfilled.

The opposing east and west coastlines bring with them very different precipitation climates. The easterly trade winds that blow in from the Indian Ocean side are laden with moisture and bring with them plentiful supplies of warm fresh rain. These winds ensure that the KwaZulu-Natal and Eastern Cape and into the Transvaal have a good supply of water, and within the Drakensberg range huge herds of dairy cattle enjoy the lush grasses irrigated by waters that filter down from the mountains.

There is a great shortage of water in most other parts of South Africa. The western side has wet winter and spring months but the summer and autumn months are dry and arid. It is at this time when irrigation is fundamental, especially for agriculture. The single largest consumer of water is irrigation, therefore water needs to be either piped into these areas or bored and stored, and there are many modern technological or commercial ventures being considered to increase and equalize water availability. This is, of course, not a new problem; archaeological finds have shown that early tribes in the Kalahari Desert used ostrich shells for storing and carrying water, and would migrate to follow seasonal rainfall.

## WINE

The South African wine industry began under the command and guidance of commander Jan Van Rieebeck, and the first vintage was uncorked on 2 February 1659. The Cape was known as the tavern of the seas around this time, as it was essentially an outpost to refresh depleted ships and their crews, and the quality of the wine was poor. Between 1680 and 1690, however, vineyards came under the highly beneficial influence of the Huguenots, French Protestants who were exiled from France and arrived with valuable knowledge and experience of top-quality viticulture.

Another huge influence on the establishment of South African wine was the first governor of the Cape from 1691 to 1699, Simon Van der Stel. Van der Stel developed an area in the Constantia Valley that he decided should be the site of South Africa's first vineyards. By the late harvesting of very ripe grapes he produced a wine known as Constantia, which proved so popular it became one of the most famous sweet wines drunk in the courts and at the banquet tables of Europe. It later became known as the Grand Constance.

Early attempts at making wine in the region, however, were met with great challenges. A shortage of French oak, the variety of terrain, and disagreements over which vines to cultivate were all significant teething problems. A marked upturn in South African wine came in the 19th century when the British were at war with the French and a trade embargo was in place. This meant that Britain started importing wines from other producing regions of the world. At the time the British also had a controlling stake in the Cape, and so purchasing South African wine made sense.

Most of South Africa's wine is now produced in the Western Cape, which has unique growing conditions close to the equator, surrounded by mountain peaks that give shelter from the wind and too much sun, and with low humidity. The familiar Dutch white-gabled farmhouses dotted around the countryside were originally designed and erected between 1750 and 1840. Many of these houses depicted the extravagance of the VOC and the establishment of Cape Town's ports. The houses are now used in the vineyards as guest quarters, tasting rooms and restaurants, as a visit to a South African winery to taste and experience the produce has now become part of the must-do list on tours of the country.

**Stellenbosch.**

**Groot Constantia vineyard.**

**Directions to the nearest source of water.**

# BUSH FOOD AND BRAAIS ...

*... the cornerstone of South Africa's culinary tradition is cooking in the great outdoors.*

The legacy of sharing food around a campfire was passed down from the indigenous herders of the Kohi, to the Dutch, to the Cape Malays with their sosaties and bredes, then on to the aspiring cooks and chefs of the 21st century. There is a great social joy attached to cooking outdoors, and no finer way to eat dinner than sitting in the golden hours of a summer evening on a west-facing stoop, watching the sun dip below the Veld.

South African braai experts prefer wood as a fuel rather than charcoal – arguing that the smoke and white heat gives the meat a unique flavour – although searing meat on flat, hot stones has become popular, which is truly going back to how it was once done in the pre-colonial era. There is also a wide range of commercial outdoor ovens and gas-fired plates to choose from, but for the purist nothing beats a smoky campfire.

*Pot bread is classic South African food, devised when necessity was the mother of invention.*

# BRAAI-BAKED POT BREAD

Dutch trekkers cooked all their food on a camp fire, and this recipe cleverly makes a miniature oven out of a pot. It is important that you have a good cast-iron pot with a tightly-fitting lid. The bottom will be in direct contact with the heat, so the bread is often slightly darker on one side. This recipe uses wheat flour from the wonderful Eureka mills who use wheat grown in Swartland in an environmentally low-impact way.

**Makes a 1kg/2¼lb loaf**

500g/1¼lb/4½ cups strong
white bread flour
10ml/2 tsp salt
10ml/2 tsp fast-acting dry yeast
10ml/2 tsp white sugar
30ml/2 tbsp olive oil
butter, for greasing
1 egg, beaten

**1** Sift the flour and salt into a large mixing bowl. Mix the yeast and sugar together in a small bowl and add a little lukewarm water to make a paste.

**2** Make a well in the centre of the flour and add the yeast and sugar paste and olive oil, mix in and then gradually add 300ml/½ pint/1¼ cups cold water until you have a soft dough. You might not need all the water. Knead on an oiled work surface for 10 minutes until the dough is soft, smooth and silky. This could be done with the dough hook attachment of a food processor. Place in a lightly oiled bowl and cover with a damp dish towel or oiled clear film (plastic wrap).

**3** At this stage you could leave your dough overnight in the refrigerator to slowly prove, or in a warm place for 1 hour.

**4** When the dough has doubled in size, tip out on to a lightly floured surface and knock back (punch down) the dough. Knead for 5–10 minutes to help develop the gluten in the flour, then form into a ball. Grease the inside of the pot, and the lid, with butter. Ensure that there is enough space for the dough to grow and rise within the pot. Place the dough inside the pot, cover and leave in a warm place for about 20–25 minutes. If using an oven, preheat to 180°C/350°F/Gas 4, or light the braai or campfire.

**5** When the loaf has doubled in size, brush the top with the beaten egg. Make sure the flames on the braai or fire have died down and the coals or logs are white hot, and place the pot on top. You need to move the pot around the fire throughout the cooking time, so the heat is not too intense on one part of the pot, and the bread cooks evenly. If cooking in the oven, place the pot inside and bake for 30–35 minutes.

**6** Check the bread is cooked by tapping the top: if it sounds hollow, remove from the pot and turn out on to a wire rack. Cool for at least 30 minutes. Slice while warm and spread generously with fresh butter. This bread makes a lovely accompaniment to any South African soup or casserole.

*Cook's tip* Placing the dough in the refrigerator overnight slows down the proving process and develops the flavour of the bread. You can experiment with various toppings on the pot bread; poppy or pumpkin seeds give a lovely crunchy texture.

Here the fish is basted with a little sweet apricot jam ...

# SNOEK, MEALIES AND POTATOES ON THE BRAAI

This simple dish uses a fish that wrestles with the ice-cold waters of the Southern Ocean and is lean and firm. Ask your fishmonger to butterfly the fish; removing the head and backbone without separating the fillets. Fresh corn cobs are called green mealies in South Africa, and are the perfect accompaniment to the snoek.

**Serves 4**

75ml/2½fl oz/⅓ cup apricot jam (see page 148)

15ml/1 tbsp Worcestershire sauce

4 corn cobs, trimmed but with the leaves left on

1 whole snoek or hake, about 2kg/4½lb, cleaned, head and backbone removed

50g/2oz butter

salt and black pepper

cherry tomatoes and spring onions (scallions), roasted, to serve

**For the chilli butter**

75g/3oz butter, softened

1–2 red chillies, deseeded and very finely chopped

45ml/3 tbsp chopped fresh coriander (cilantro)

30ml/2 tbsp chopped fresh parsley

**For the sweet potatoes**

4 medium sweet potatoes, washed

45ml/4 tbsp clear honey

30ml/2 tbsp butter

**1** To make the chilli butter, place all the ingredients in a mixing bowl. Use an electric hand whisk or fork to bring together and combine. Season with salt and pepper. Place on to a sheet of baking parchment and shape into a long cylinder. Roll up like a sausage and place in the freezer. Remove from the freezer 20 minutes before serving, to soften slightly.

**2** Prepare and light the braai. When the flames have died down it is ready. Place each sweet potato on a square sheet of buttered foil, drizzle with honey and season well with salt and pepper. Seal the foil and place the parcels on to the embers of the fire. Turn every so often to ensure even cooking, test with a skewer after 35–40 minutes, and when tender move to the edge of the braai.

**3** Meanwhile place the jam and Worcestershire sauce in a small pan on the side of the braai and allow the jam to warm a little. At this stage you can add the corn on to the edges of the hot braai. Cook for 12–15 minutes until the outside is black but the corn kernels are tender. Peel the leaves back and insert a small sharp knife in a kernel to test.

**4** Now cook the fish. Butter a large, doubled, sheet of foil, big enough to hold the fish. Place the fish on the foil, skin side down, and lift the foil on to the hot braai. Cook for about 4–5 minutes basting from time to time with the warm jam. Turn over and cook the other side, brushing the jam mixture on to the fish as it roasts. Remove and set aside to rest for a few minutes.

**5** Serve the fish with a peeled mealie topped with some chilli butter, and a sweet potato, accompanied by some cherry tomatoes and spring onions.

# GRILLED YELLOWTAIL IN BANANA LEAF

Although most of South Africa doesn't have the tropical climate necessary for banana cultivation, they are grown successfully in the sub-tropical region of KwaZulu-Natal, where they are used in savoury as well as sweet dishes. Banana leaves not only seal in the moisture and flavour of the fish, they also add a cooling, lightly fragrant taste. They can be found in Asian stores and supermarkets, and can easily be frozen. If you can't find yellowtail fish fillets, they could be substituted with snoek, sea bass or snapper.

**Serves 4**

3 cloves garlic, peeled
5cm/2½in piece root ginger
2 red chillies, deseeded and finely chopped
1 stick lemon grass, trimmed
30ml/2 tbsp chopped fresh coriander (cilantro), leaves and stalks
30ml/2 tbsp groundnut (peanut) oil
3 limes
4 banana leaves
4 x skinless white fish fillets, about 200g/7oz each
120ml/8 tbsp coconut cream
salt and black pepper
steamed jasmine rice, and banana sambal (see page 119), to serve

**1** Grind the garlic, ginger, chillies, lemon grass, coriander, groundnut oil and the finely grated zest and the juice of 1 lime in a pestle and mortar, or pulse in a food processor to form a paste. Transfer to an airtight container.

**2** Preheat a grill (broiler) or braai. Trim the banana leaves into squares measuring 30cm/12in. To soften the banana leaves, pass one side of the leaf over an open flame for five seconds. Slice each of the limes into 6 slices.

**3** Place 3 slices of limes in the centre of each banana leaf. Lay a fish fillet on top of the limes. Season with salt and pepper.

**4** Smear 30ml/2 tbsp of the spice paste on top of the fish. Any leftover paste can be kept in the refrigerator for up to five days. Pour 30ml/2 tbsp coconut cream over each fillet, then fold the 4 sides of the leaves over and secure well with butcher's string.

**5** Place the parcels on the grill, with the lime side of the parcel in contact with the grill, for 8–10 minutes; the cooking time will depend on the thickness of the fish. Remove from the grill and serve with steamed rice and banana sambal.

The migrating yellowtail fish, which swims in the warm sub-tropical waters around Natal and the Eastern Cape, has delicious firm, meaty flesh.

# BEER CAN PERI-PERI CHICKEN

Cooking chicken on a can of beer means that the beer creates an alcoholic steam that gives a deliciously tender result. Brining the chicken before it's cooked also helps the meat stay moist, but you can omit this stage if you wish.

**Serves 4–5**

150g/5oz/¾ cup sea salt
6 allspice berries
1 bay leaf
5ml/1 tsp chilli flakes
2.5ml/½ tsp black peppercorns
1 medium free-range chicken, about 2kg/4½lb in weight
1 large can good quality light beer
salt and black pepper
lemon wedges, to serve

**For the peri-peri sauce**
8 red bird's eye chillies, stalks trimmed
6 cloves garlic, peeled and roughly chopped
5ml/1 tsp sea salt flakes
5ml/1 tsp fresh oregano
10ml/2 tsp hot chilli powder, or to taste
100ml/3½fl oz/scant ½ cup good quality olive oil
30ml/2 tbsp red wine vinegar
juice of 2 lemons
45ml/3 tbsp fresh parsley

**1** To brine the chicken, place the salt and spices in a large pan together with 2 litres/3½ pints/8 cups cold water. Bring to the boil to dissolve the salt, then remove from the heat and allow to cool. When cooled, immerse the chicken in the brine and allow to sit there for 4–6 hours, turning once.

**2** While the chicken is brining, prepare the peri-peri sauce by placing all the ingredients in a food processor and blitzing until the chillies and garlic are finely chopped and the sauce has slightly emulsified.

**3** Meanwhile prepare the braai. When the coals are white hot the braai is ready. Alternatively preheat the oven to 200°C/400°F/Gas 5.

**4** Remove the chicken from the brine and pat dry. Open the beer can, take a good swig so that it isn't full, and set the can on the work surface. Place the chicken on top, and push down, so that most of the can is inside the cavity.

**5** Set the chicken can-side down on to a roasting pan lined with a double sheet of tin foil. Take 2 large sheets of foil and place either side of the pan, tucking it well into the rim, allow the foil to cover the chicken to make a tent and scrunch together in the middle. Place on the grill and cook for 15–20 minutes, remove and brush with a little more of the peri-peri sauce.

**6** Cook for a further 45–50 minutes adding more fuel to the braai to keep a constant temperature. Check the chicken is done by inserting a skewer into the chicken's leg between the thigh and drumstick, if the juices run clear then it is ready. Liberally brush with more peri-peri sauce, carefully remove the can and then place the chicken directly on the braai for a few minutes on all sides to crisp up the skin. Serve with lemon wedges and a green salad.

# THE BURGER

**Serves 6**

500g/1¼lb/2½ cups minced (ground) pork shoulder
500g/1¼lb/2½ cups minced (ground) beef
30ml/2 tbsp breadcrumbs
15ml/1 tbsp ground coriander
2.5ml/½ tsp ground nutmeg
2.5ml/½ tsp ground cloves
mature (sharp) Cheddar cheese, sliced
salt and black pepper
6 burger buns, sliced in half
olive oil, for drizzling
iceberg lettuce, finely shredded,
2 large vine-ripened tomatoes, sliced, and tomato chutney (see page 114), to serve

**For the pickled cucumbers**

2 large cucumbers, washed, partially peeled, and thinly sliced
1 small onion, thinly sliced
25g/1oz sea salt flakes
100ml/3½fl oz/scant ½ cup white wine vinegar
50g/2oz/¼ cup soft brown sugar
1 dried chilli, crumbled
2 cloves
2.5ml/½ tsp fennel seeds
2.5ml/½ tsp coriander seeds
5 black peppercorns

Travelling around South Africa, eating in a variety of places, you will notice a recurring menu item: the South African take on the burger. It may not be sophisticated food nor is it steeped in an African heritage, but from gourmet restaurants to pop-up cafes it is one of the nation's favourite foods.

**1** To make the pickled cucumbers, prepare your jars by sterilizing in the dishwasher, then keep warm in a low oven. Place the sliced cucumber and onion in a colander. Sprinkle with salt, mix well and set aside for about one hour, then rinse under cold water and leave to drain.

**2** Heat the vinegar, sugar, chilli, cloves, fennel, coriander and peppercorns in a medium pan. When the sugar has dissolved turn the heat up and add the drained cucumbers, cook for 1 minute and then decant, with the liquid, into the warm jars. Seal, cool completely, then chill in the refrigerator. The cucumbers will keep for up to 2 weeks.

**3** To make the burgers, place the beef and pork into a large mixing bowl. Add the breadcrumbs, spices, 2.5ml/½ tsp salt, and plenty of pepper. Mix well until all the spices are well incorporated.

**4** Divide the meat into 6 equal-sized patties. Set aside in the refrigerator to firm up until ready to cook. Prepare the braai; when the fuel is white hot, brush the burgers with a little olive oil on both sides to avoid them sticking, season both sides with salt and pepper and place on the grill. Cook for 5–6 minutes, turning every 25 seconds, and when cooked top with a slice of cheese.

**5** Drizzle a little olive oil on each bun and place cut side down on to the braai to toast for about 1 minute. To serve, place some shredded lettuce on the bottom layer of each bun, add a burger and place sliced tomato, pickled cucumber and a spoonful of chutney on top.

# PREGO ROLL

Portuguese food has ingrained itself into the South African diet since the 1950s, when hard-working immigrants came from Portugal to work in South Africa's gold and platinum mines. This delicious snack may be simple, but can't be rushed. It uses rump steak, which is a little chewier than fillet, and unusually it is flavoured with coffee.

**Serves 2**

300g/11oz rump steak, trimmed and divided into two
120ml/4fl oz/½ cup South African red wine
2 sprigs fresh rosemary, leaves chopped
1 fresh bay leaf, bruised
2.5ml/½ tsp dried oregano
3 cloves garlic, crushed
5ml/1 tsp dried chilli flakes
5ml/1 tsp ground espresso coffee
olive oil, 2 bread rolls and lemon wedges, to serve

**For the tomatoes**

150g/5oz cherry tomatoes, halved
1 small red chilli, seeded and finely chopped
5ml/1 tsp red wine vinegar
30ml/2tbsp olive oil
sea salt flakes and black pepper

**1** Place each piece of steak between 2 sheets of clear film (plastic wrap) and flatten lightly with a cutlet bat, or rolling pin, to tenderize the meat. Place the steaks on a wide serving dish and add the red wine, rosemary, bay leaf, oregano, garlic, chilli flakes and coffee. Place in the refrigerator and leave to marinate for at least 6 hours or overnight if possible, turning from time to time.

**2** Preheat a braai to very hot, making sure that the wood or coal is in the middle of the cooking area.

**3** Mix the tomatoes, chilli, vinegar, and olive oil in a small bowl. Add some salt and pepper and set aside somewhere warm to marinate for 30 minutes.

**4** When the flames on the braai have died down, remove the steaks from the dish, reserving the marinade. Pat the steaks dry, season with salt and pepper and rub 15ml/1 tbsp oil into each one. Place on the grill, over the centre of the fuel, and cook for 3–4 minutes, turning every 25 seconds until they are cooked to your liking. Remove the steaks from the heat and set aside to rest.

**5** Take the reserved marinade and tip it into a hot frying pan, place on the braai and reduce for 5 minutes until thick and syrupy. Add in any of the meaty juices that have come out of the steaks.

**6** Drizzle the insides of the rolls with a little olive oil, and scorch a little on the braai. Place a piece of steak inside, top with a little reduced marinade and serve with some of the marinated tomatoes and lemon wedges.

# BOEREWORS WITH TOMATO SAUCE

Classic South African boerewors are a great example of the marriage of European influences and superb local produce. Dutch and German settlers supplied sausage-making skills, putting every part of the slaughtered carcass to good use, while coriander seeds, nutmeg and allspice from the East Indies are added as flavourings.

**Serves 8**

10m/30ft sausage, or hog casings, 36mm/1¼in width
1kg/2¼lb chuck beef steak
500g/1¼lb pork belly, skin removed
15ml/1 tbsp coriander seeds
15ml/1 tbsp black peppercorns
2.5ml/½ tsp allspice berries
2.5ml/½ tsp grated nutmeg
7.5ml/1½ tsp demerara (raw) sugar
75ml/2½fl oz/⅓ cup South African Shiraz or similar red wine
30ml/2 tbsp salt
45ml/3 tbsp breadcrumbs
crusty bread rolls, to serve

**For the tomato sauce**
6 medium vine-ripened tomatoes
30ml/2 tbsp olive oil
2 onions, finely chopped
3 cloves garlic, crushed
5ml/1 tsp chopped fresh marjoram
15ml/1 tbsp red wine vinegar
15ml/1 tbsp sugar
30ml/2 tbsp chopped fresh parsley
pinch chilli flakes
salt and pepper

**1** Soak the casings in warm water to soften, then rinse. Your casings may be spooled, which makes them easier to attach to the machine.

**2** Take the beef and pork and mince (grind) it through the coarse setting on a mincer (grinder) into a large bowl. You could ask your butcher to do this.

**3** In a frying pan, gently dry-fry the coriander seeds, peppercorns and allspice berries for 1–2 minutes to lightly toast and release their oils. Tip into a mortar and grind to a powder with a pestle. Add to the ground meat; together with the nutmeg, sugar, red wine, salt and breadcrumbs. Mix well with your hands.

**4** Fit one edge of the casing on to the nozzle of the sausage stuffing machine and tie a small knot in the end. Slowly add the sausage meat in a steady stream, gently moulding it with your hands to make sure it is packed firmly and there are no gaps or bulges. Twist each sausage into links or into coils. Prick any air pockets with a pin or skewer. Chill until ready to use so the sausages have time to settle and firm up.

**5** To make the tomato sauce, light the braai and roast the tomatoes on the grill until the skins begin to blister, or roast in the oven with a drizzle of olive oil. When cool enough to handle, peel off the skins and scoop out the seeds. Roughly chop the flesh.

**6** Heat the olive oil in a medium pan, add the onions and cook gently for 5 minutes until soft but translucent. Add the garlic and cook for a further 2 minutes. Add the marjoram and chopped tomatoes. Cover and cook for 15 minutes until the sauce has reduced. Add the vinegar and sugar, stir in the parsley and chilli flakes, and season with salt and pepper.

**7** Prepare your braai. When the coals on the braai are white-hot and all the flames have died down, cook the coils of boerewors for about 10–15 minutes, until the skins are dark and the centre is still slightly pink. Serve the hot sausages stuffed inside some griddled rolls, topped with tomato relish.

*Cook's tip* Casings are widely available online or from local butchers, and you can fill them by hand using a piping bag, or buy an inexpensive sausage maker like the one we used here. Natural casings come in various widths, and for thick sausages like boerewors, and for sausage-making beginners, a 'hog' casing is probably the best choice.

# STEAK WITH MONKEY GLAND SAUCE

There are great farmers to be found all over South Africa who are producing outstanding veld-reared animals, like Angus McIntosh, who cross-breeds Angus and Limousine cattle at Spier farm in Stellenbosch. This recipe uses a cut called 'côte de boeuf', which contains bone to aid flavour and juiciness. The sauce gets its name from a 19th-century theory that monkey glands made men virile, and alludes to the sauce's macho fiery heat.

**Serves 4–6**

2 x 500g/1¼lb côte de boeuf (rib-eye on the bone) steaks, trimmed
sea salt flakes and black pepper

**For the monkey gland sauce**
30ml/2 tbsp olive oil
15ml/1 tbsp butter
2 medium onions, finely chopped
2 cloves garlic, crushed
1 x 400g can chopped tomatoes
15ml/1 tbsp Worcestershire sauce
45ml/3 tbsp brandy
15ml/1 tbsp soy sauce
150ml/¼ pint/⅔ cup Mrs Ball's chilli chutney, or sweet chilli sauce
30ml/2 tbsp white sugar
30ml/2 tbsp red wine vinegar

**For the gremolata**
30ml/2 tbsp fresh chopped parsley
5ml/1 tsp chopped fresh sage
5ml/1 tsp chopped fresh rosemary
5ml/1 tsp fresh thyme leaves
3 large cloves garlic, crushed
finely grated zest of 1 lemon
10ml/2 tsp olive oil

**1** Make the sauce by heating the oil in a medium pan. When the oil is hot add the butter and allow to sizzle a little before adding the onions. Cook, stirring, for 5 minutes until soft and translucent. Add the garlic and cook for a minute.

**2** Add the tomatoes to the pan and cook for 10 minutes until they start to break down slightly. Add the rest of the sauce ingredients and season with a little salt and pepper. Lower the heat to a gentle simmer and place a lid on. Cook for 45 minutes until the sauce is thick and reduced and the tomatoes have broken down. Check for seasoning and keep in a warm place.

**3** Prepare and light the braai. Remove the meat from the refrigerator about half an hour before you are going to cook it.

**4** Season the steaks with a little salt on both sides. Make sure your fire has a steady high heat, the flames have died down and the wood or coals are white hot, then carefully place your steaks on to the fire, count to 25 seconds and turn. Repeat this until the internal temperature of the meat reaches 50°C/120°F for rare, 55°C/130°F for medium rare and 60°C/140°F for medium, about 15–20 minutes. The time will depend on the thickness of the steaks.

**5** Remove the steaks from the grill and set aside, covered, in a warm place to rest, turning regularly while resting. Mix all the ingredients for the gremolata in a small mixing bowl.

**6** When ready to eat, smear the cooked steak on both sides with the gremolata, then cut the steak into thin slices. Serve with the warm monkey gland sauce.

*Cook's tip* The great food scientist and part-time cook Harold McGee did numerous tests on cooking steak, amongst other things. He concludes that meat should be turned on the braai every 25 seconds to ensure the meat receives even pulses of heat that prevent it from overcooking on one side.

*Cooks beautifully on a braai ...*

The Great Karoo was once an almost impenetrable barrier, and early settlers and explorers on the way to the Highveld denounced it as a frightening place of great heat, great frosts, great floods and great droughts.

# KAROO LAMB WITH LAVENDER

The Klein Karoo region is a semi-arid area with underground water that makes it arable, and despite its inhospitable terrain and climate, a particular hardy breed of sheep, the Karoo, can withstand the region's frosty winters and blisteringly hot summers. Among the people who live in the area there is a strong tradition of hospitality that goes back to the days of the Voortrekkers, and tired travellers will often be invited to drink a cup of coffee on a shady stoop.

**Serves 8**

30ml/2 tbsp olive oil

1 whole leg lamb or mutton, weighing about 2kg/4½lb

12 sprigs fresh rosemary, plus 1 large branch

4 large garlic cloves, sliced into thin slivers

8 sprigs fresh lavender

a little red wine and stock, to deglaze

smoked sea salt and pepper

**1** Prepare the braai. Rub the olive oil into the skin of the lamb. When the flames have died down to a steady heat, add the rosemary branch to the fire and place the lamb on to a rack on the fire. Brown on all sides making sure the skin is crisp and golden. You can also do this on a large roasting pan over an open flame or stove top.

**2** When your meat is seared, transfer to a chopping board. Preheat your oven to just 90°C/195°F/Gas ¼. With a small knife, make small incisions into the lamb. Stuff the holes with a little garlic, rosemary and lavender heads. Place some of the rosemary and lavender sprigs on to the base of a heavy roasting pan.

**3** Place the lamb on top of the herbs, pour 150ml/¼ pint/⅔ cup water into the bottom of the pan and roast for 2–2½ hours. Remove from the oven and allow the meat to rest for about ½ an hour.

**4** To carve the meat, slice it towards the bone and remove each large lobe of meat, then carve these chunks across the grain into generous slices. Season each slice with salt and pepper.

**5** Place the roasting pan on a medium heat and bring the juices to a boil, deglaze the pan with a splash of red wine, and scrape any residue on the bottom into the juices. Add some stock, if you wish, and serve the lamb with the juices poured over.

*Karoo lamb is a special treat, said to have a unique flavour from the wild shrubs and flowers that grow there.*

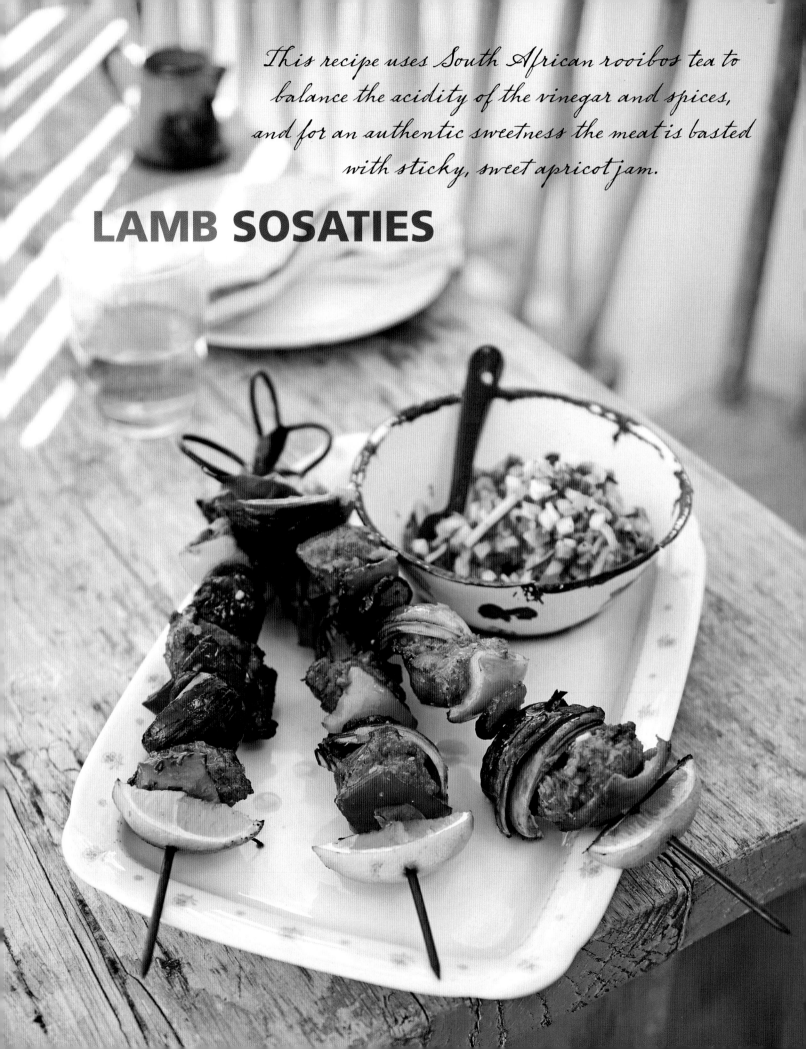

*This recipe uses South African rooibos tea to balance the acidity of the vinegar and spices, and for an authentic sweetness the meat is basted with sticky, sweet apricot jam.*

# LAMB SOSATIES

Sosaties are of Malaysian origin where they are called 'sesates', meaning spicy skewered meats, usually lamb, and they are ideal prepare-ahead food for a braai. Sosaties can be cooked over the coals in a few minutes, giving fast food to a hungry gathering. The meat can be marinated in airtight bags and kept in the refrigerator for up to two days. Use metal skewers if you have them, as they are more robust on the flames.

**Serves 4**

1kg/2¼lb lamb leg steaks or neck fillet cut into 3cm/1½in cubes

20 dried apricots

red or yellow (bell) peppers cut into 3cm/1½in cubes

3 red onions, peeled and quartered

16 small fresh bay leaves

2 lemons, cut into quarters

salt and black pepper

8 metal skewers

papaya sambal, finely chopped (see page 119), to serve

**For the marinade**

15ml/1 tbsp sunflower oil

3 red onions, finely grated

5cm/2in piece fresh ginger, peeled and grated

3 cloves garlic, crushed

3 red chillies, finely chopped

15ml/1 tbsp medium curry powder

225g/8oz/1 cup apricot jam (see page 148)

100ml/3½fl oz/scant ½ cup malt vinegar

250ml/8fl oz/1 cup rooibos tea, strong infusion

**1** First make the marinade. Heat a pan over a medium heat, add the oil and grated onion and cook, stirring all the time, for 3–4 minutes without allowing the onion to colour.

**2** Add the ginger, garlic, chillies and curry powder to the pan and cook for 2–3 minutes. Stir in the jam, vinegar and rooibos tea. Bring to a simmer and cook gently for 5 minutes until thick and slightly reduced. Transfer to a large bowl and set aside to cool.

**3** When the marinade is completely cooled, add the cubed lamb and leave to marinate for about 12 hours or overnight; not only will the meat become flavoursome but it will also be tenderized.

**4** Prepare the braai. Thread the pieces of meat on to the skewers, alternating each piece with either a piece of apricot, pepper or red onion. Use the bay leaves and lemons as bookends for each skewer.

**5** When the flames have died down and the coal or wood is white hot, place the skewers on the braai and cook for 6–8 minutes, turning regularly to ensure even cooking; be careful as the apricots will colour very quickly, and could scorch.

**6** When cooked, remove the skewers from the braai and rest for 5 minutes, before serving with papaya sambal.

*Cook's tip* Rooibos bushes grow in the Western Cape province, and its red leaves (rooibos means 'red bush' in Old Dutch) are used to make a herbal tea that has been popular among all South Africans for generations. The tea is now becoming well known around the world, appreciated for its high level of antioxidants and lack of caffeine.

# KAROO OSTRICH POTJIE

This dish is campfire cookery at its finest, creating a slow cooking potjie that is perfect for eating under the stars of the clear-sky Great Karoo. A potjie or potjiekos is a three-legged, round-bodied cast iron pot that arrived in South Africa with the Dutch settlers. Still used in bush camps or traditional South African homes, they have become in vogue again with the growth of the slow food movement.

**Serves 6–8**

2kg/4½lb ostrich neck cut into 6cm/3in pieces (ask the butcher to do this)
50g/2oz/½ cup plain (all-purpose) flour
45ml/3 tbsp vegetable oil
175g/6oz/1 cup smoked bacon or pancetta lardons
225g/8oz/3 cups button (white) mushrooms, quartered
5ml/1 tsp ground ginger
5ml/1 tsp garam masala
30ml/2 tbsp tomato purée (paste)
finely grated zest of 1 small orange
500ml/17fl oz/generous 2 cups hot beef stock
salt and black pepper
crusty bread, to serve

**For the marinade**
750ml/1¼ pints/3 cups full-bodied red wine
4 sprigs fresh thyme
2 bay leaves
5ml/1 tsp allspice berries
4 large onions, peeled and sliced
1 head of garlic, halved crossways
4 large carrots, peeled and chopped
3 sticks celery, sliced

**1** The meat should be marinated for 24 hours, so on the day before cooking place the wine, herbs, spices, onions, garlic, carrots and celery into a large bowl and add the ostrich meat. Cover and chill overnight.

**2** Remove the meat from the marinade and pat dry with kitchen paper. Strain the marinade through a colander, reserving the liquid and the vegetables in separate bowls. If using an oven, preheat it to 140°C/275°F/Gas 1, or prepare the campfire or braai.

**3** Dip the meat in flour on all sides, and pat off the excess. Heat 15ml/1 tbsp of the oil in a large frying pan over a medium heat and cook the meat in batches until browned on all sides. Remove from the pan and add to the potjie. Deglaze the frying pan with the liquid from the marinade, simmer for a couple of minutes and then pour into the potjie.

**4** Heat 15ml/1 tbsp oil in a large pan. Add all the vegetables from the marinade and mushrooms and cook, stirring, for 10 minutes until the vegetables are slightly coloured. Stir in the ground ginger and garam masala, tomato purée and grated orange zest. Cook, stirring, for another 2 minutes.

**5** Transfer the cooked vegetables to the potjie, and add the hot stock. Cover the potjie with its lid, and cook on the edge of the fire or in the oven for 2½–3 hours until the meat is tender. Keep turning the pot if cooking on a fire and maintain the glowing embers. If the liquid evaporates too quickly during cooking from the potjie, add a little more stock or water.

**6** Remove the potjie from the heat and allow to stand for about 10 minutes before serving. Serve with pumpkin bread to mop up the juices.

*The dish will taste even better if made the day before, then slowly reheated.*

*Oudtshoorn in Klein Karoo is a region known principally for ostrich farming — and racing!*

*Cooking outside is a much-loved South African tradition.*

# FISH AND SHELLFISH ...

*... in South Africa seafood is almost always cooked on the braai.*

On arrival in what would become Cape Town, the first colonial settlers encountered a nomadic people who lived a simple existence along the coastline, collecting shellfish and cooking them on hot coals. Europeans continued the tradition, but gradually added their own twists, such as basting their fish with herby butters, or with blatjang, which the Indonesians brought from Java, to give the flesh a sweet and sticky glaze. Cape Malays served spicy fish curries with crisp, fresh sambals to give a cool contrast, while the Portuguese introduced hot and sharp peri-peri marinades for the sweet, warm-water grilled prawns.

# SNOEK SAMBAL

**Serves 4**

200g/7oz cooked or smoked snoek or mackerel, bones and skin removed

100g/4oz butter, melted

3 medium cloves garlic, crushed

2 red chillies, deseeded and finely chopped

grated zest and juice of 1 lemon

30ml/2 tbsp chopped fresh coriander (cilantro) leaves and stalks

15ml/1 tbsp chopped chives

salt and black pepper

**For the garlic Melba toast**

4 slices sourdough bread

1 clove garlic, crushed

45ml/3 tbsp olive oil

5ml/1 tsp each of chopped fresh thyme and rosemary

**For the pomegranate sambal**

150g/5oz/1 cup pomegranate seeds

1 green chilli, deseeded and finely chopped

30ml/2 tbsp fresh chopped coriander (cilantro)

½ small red onion, finely chopped

juice of 1 lemon

1 small cucumber, peeled, seeded and finely chopped

It is thought that Malay slaves brought fish sambal to South Africa at the end of the 17th century, but here it is served with pomegranate sambal, a more modern accompaniment. Though not indigenous to South Africa, pomegranates have been grown with great success in places like Klein Karoo, and the North and Western Cape.

**1** Place the snoek and melted butter into a food processor, and pulse until smooth. Transfer to a medium bowl, fold in the garlic, chilli, lemon juice, fresh coriander and chives. Season well to taste, adding a little more lemon juice if you wish. Cover and chill until required for up to 3 days.

**2** Prepare the braai or preheat a griddle. To make the Melba toast, rub the slices of bread with a cut clove of garlic, then drizzle a little olive oil on both sides of the bread. Toast on the braai on each side until crisp and golden. While still warm, slice the toast in half horizontally to make 8 thin slices.

**3** Mix the remaining oil with the crushed garlic, thyme and rosemary. Drizzle the garlic oil over the untoasted sides of the bread and toast again on the grill until crisp. Cut into elegant triangles and set aside until ready to serve.

**4** To make the pomegranate sambal, place all the ingredients in a bowl and mix together. Transfer to a serving bowl. Spread the garlic Melba toast with snoek sambal and serve with pomegranate sambal.

*Spread on crisp Melba toast, this sambal makes a simple appetizer for an evening meal.*

# PLETTENBERG BAY SQUID

We used lovely small, tender squid caught in Plettenberg Bay for this recipe. Make sure that the outer skin-like membrane is removed before cooking. Soaking the squid in milk helps tenderize the flesh. The nut oil used for frying the squid needs to be made in advance so that the flavour develops.

**Serves 4**

500g/1¼lb small squid, quills and ink sacks removed

500ml/17fl oz/generous 2 cups milk

2 red onions, thinly sliced

2 red (bell) peppers, trimmed and cut into thin strips

4 cloves garlic, crushed

5 medium tomatoes, skinned, seeded and chopped

250g/9oz fresh spinach, washed and shredded

30ml/2 tbsp Mrs Balls' chilli chutney or similar

salt and black pepper

### For the nut oil

1 litre/1¾ pints/4 cups good quality groundnut (peanut) oil

250g/9oz/2 cups nuts such as walnuts, hazelnuts or almonds

1 large sprig fresh rosemary

1 large sprig fresh thyme

**1** To make the nut oil, dry roast the nuts in a large frying pan on a low heat. Keep shaking the pan to move the nuts around, and keep an eye on them to prevent scorching. When golden, remove the nuts from the heat and allow to cool completely. Transfer to a large jar, push in the herbs and pour in the oil. Leave in a cool, dark place for up to 3 weeks.

**2** To prepare the squid, wash thoroughly in plenty of cold water, removing any remaining ink and sand. Trim off any skin from the main body of the squid and cut into even squares; make a scored little crosshatch pattern if you desire. Trim the tentacles. Place the prepared squid into the milk, ensuring it is well submerged. Cover and place in the refrigerator for an hour.

**3** Drain the squid and pat dry on kitchen paper. Discard the milk. Heat 45ml/ 3 tbsp of the nut oil over a high heat in a large wok. Add the squid and flash fry for a minute until it is golden around the edges.

**4** Add the onions, pepper and garlic to the wok and cook for 2–3 minutes. Add the tomatoes and spinach and cook for about 1–2 minutes until the spinach starts to wilt.

**5** Add the chilli chutney to the wok, mix, then season well with salt and black pepper. Serve straight away in small bowls.

*This is a simple dish using the fine fresh local squid.*

Paternoster is one of the oldest fishing villages on the west coast, famous for its lobster and white-washed cottages.

# PERI-PERI CRAYFISH

The most famous catch in the Paternoster area is the sought-after crayfish, known locally as 'kreef'. These small spiny lobster are a real delicacy, and are the subject of much debate due to their scarcity and the fact that they are heavily poached and sold on the black market. A phenomenon known as the red tide, when algae grows and blooms at such a rate it turns the sea red, often sees the oxygen-starved crayfish march out of the water on to local beaches.

**Serves 4–6**

2 live crayfish or 1 lobster

45ml/3 tbsp melted butter

salt and black pepper and cayenne pepper, to taste

lemon wedges and a little melted butter, to serve

**For the peri-peri sauce**

30ml/2 tbsp vegetable oil

3 cloves garlic, peeled and sliced into thin slivers

1 red, 1 yellow, and 1 green (bell) pepper, seeded and finely chopped

100ml/3½fl oz/scant ½ cup peri-peri oil

30ml/2 tbsp finely chopped fresh parsley

5ml/1 tsp finely chopped fresh marjoram

juice of 1 lemon

**1** Place the crayfish in the freezer for a couple of hours before cooking, as this makes them easier to process. Preheat the grill (broiler) or braai. When the flames have died down, the braai is ready.

**2** Remove the crayfish from the freezer and place on a wooden board. Push the tip of a heavy sharp blade through the back of the head, then cut the whole crayfish in half lengthways.

**3** Brush the flesh of the crayfish with the melted butter and season with a pinch of cayenne pepper, or to taste, and a little salt and black pepper.

**4** To make the peri-peri sauce, heat the vegetable oil in a medium-sized frying pan, add the garlic and cook for 1 minute stirring well. Add the chopped peppers and cook for 1 minute. Add the peri-peri oil and remove from the heat. Stir in the herbs and lemon juice and season with a little salt and cayenne pepper to taste. Set aside.

**5** When the fire is ready place the crayfish shell side down on the grill and cook for 5 minutes until the flesh is firm but still slightly opaque. Transfer to a serving plate.

**6** To serve, spoon a little melted butter over the flesh of the crayfish, add a squeeze of lemon and liberally drizzle the peri-peri sauce on the tail and into the tomalley (also called the 'mustard') in the head. Any leftover peri-peri sauce can be transferred to an airtight container and kept in the refrigerator for up to 2 weeks.

*Cook's tip* *The tomalley serves as the crayfish's liver and pancreas and is the yellow-green part found in the head. Many people consider it a delicacy, and eat it along with the white meat; it is also often used to flavour sauces and stocks. However, it is the organ that filters waste, and there is a possibility it could be contaminated with pollutants, so therefore it must be cooked properly. If it is loose or slightly liquid, it should not be eaten.*

# SNOEK KEDGEREE

**Serves 4**

200g/7oz/1 cup jasmine rice
5ml/1 tsp groundnut (peanut) oil
1 medium onion, finely chopped
2.5ml/½ tsp cumin seeds
2.5ml/½ tsp ground turmeric
350g/12oz smoked snoek or
haddock, skinned and filleted
600ml/1 pint/2½ cups milk
1 sprig fresh thyme
1 sprig fresh rosemary
3 spring onions (scallions),
thinly sliced
30ml/2 tbsp chopped fresh
coriander (cilantro)
1 large ripe avocado, stoned
(pitted) and finely diced
4 hard-boiled eggs, cooked for
6 minutes, cooled in iced water.
salt and black pepper

**For the curry sauce**
15ml/1 tbsp groundnut (peanut) oil
1 medium onion, finely chopped
2 cloves garlic, crushed
5ml/1 tsp medium curry powder
300ml/½ pint/1¼ cups hot
vegetable stock
200ml/7fl oz/scant 1 cup
coconut cream
1 medium ripe mango, peeled,
stoned (pitted) and diced
1 banana, sliced
45ml/3 tbsp crème fraîche

Brought to the Southern Cape by the Victorian English, via India, this particular recipe is adapted from London's Savoy Hotel where the dish was once served to colonial travellers. Instead of the traditional smoked haddock, however, we used smoked snoek, from the Hout Bay Snoek Smokery.

**1** Rinse the rice under plenty of cold water. Heat the oil in a medium pan over a gentle heat, add the onion and cook until soft and translucent. Add the cumin seeds, turmeric and rice and cook, stirring, for a further 1 minute. Add 400ml/14fl oz/1⅔ cups of water and a good pinch of salt, bring to a simmer, and cook, covered, for about 13–15 minutes, until all the liquid has been absorbed. Cover the pan with a clean dish towel, remove from the heat and keep warm.

**2** While the rice is cooking, place the fish in a small frying pan and cover with the milk and add the thyme and rosemary. Slowly bring to the boil. Once boiling remove from the heat and set aside to cool until you can handle the fish. Remove the fish from the milk and with your hands gently separate into bite-sized flakes. Discard the milk and the herbs.

**3** To make the curry sauce, heat the oil in a medium pan, add the chopped onion and cook for 5 minutes until soft and translucent. Add the garlic and curry powder and cook for another 2 minutes. Add the stock and cook for 5–10 minutes, add the coconut cream, and cook for a further 5 minutes. Add the mango and heat through until the mango is softened.

**4** Remove the curry sauce from the heat and add the sliced banana. Stir in the crème fraîche then use a stick blender or food processor to blend the sauce until smooth. Check for seasoning and keep warm.

**5** Add the fish flakes, spring onions, coriander and chopped avocado to the rice, fold to mix in gently then transfer to a serving plate. Quarter the boiled eggs and place on top of the rice. Serve with the warm curry sauce.

# FISH BOBOTIE

**Serves 4**

3 slices white bread

150ml/¼ pint/⅔ cup full-fat (whole) milk

15ml/1 tbsp sunflower oil

12g/½oz butter and a little extra for greasing

2 medium red onions, finely chopped

3 cloves garlic, crushed

5cm/2½in piece fresh root ginger, peeled and grated

10ml/2 tsp medium curry powder and a little extra for sprinkling

5ml/1 tsp garam masala

2.5ml/¼ tsp grated nutmeg

30ml/2 tbsp raisins

500g/1¼lb hake or other firm white fish, boned and skinned

juice of 1 lemon

8 kaffir lime leaves or lemon leaves

30ml/2 tbsp blanched almonds, roughly chopped

mango and peach atjar, to serve (see page 116)

**For the topping**

4 eggs, lightly beaten

500ml/17fl oz/generous 2 cups full-fat (whole) milk

1.5ml/¼ tsp grated nutmeg

Boboties are usually made with spiced meat mixed with raisins, nuts and a creamy egg topping. This is a lighter fish version, made here with hake, trawl-caught off the coast of Africa from the deep waters of Namibia.

**1** Soak the bread with the milk for about 20–25 minutes. Remove the bread from the milk, squeeze well and place into a large mixing bowl.

**2** Place a frying pan over a medium heat and add the oil, butter and onions. Cook, stirring, for about 5 minutes until the onions are soft and translucent. Add the garlic, ginger, curry powder, garam masala and grated nutmeg. Cook for another 1–2 minutes, stir in the raisins, then remove from the heat.

**3** Mince (grind) or finely chop the cleaned fish fillets and add to the squeezed bread, together with the spiced onions. Season with lemon juice and a little black pepper, and mix until well incorporated.

**4** Grease 4 individual ovenproof dishes or ramekins with a little butter. Sprinkle a little curry powder around the insides and bottom of each dish. Divide the mixture between the dishes, placing a couple of lime or lemon leaves in each one. Top each dish with some chopped almonds. Preheat the oven to 180°C/350°F/Gas 4.

**5** To make the topping, mix the eggs and milk together, and season with grated nutmeg and a little salt and pepper. Pour into the filled dishes and place on a baking sheet. Bake in the oven for 20–25 minutes until golden. Stand for a few minutes, before serving with mango and peach atjar.

*Boboties are said to be the national dish of South Africa ...*

# TEA-SMOKED DRAKENSBERG TROUT

It is believed that it was Scottish migrants, longing for the lochs and rivers of home, who introduced trout to the Drakensberg waterway during the 1900s. In these fast-flowing rivers the Scottish settlers could pit their wits against the trout with fly rod and reel, and it is still a popular region for fly-fishing today. In this recipe we cured the fish first to remove excess moisture and add flavour, before smoking it with a little rooibos tea. For an unusual twist the fish is served with a little lime pickle. When preparing limes always remove the centre core of pith, which can be tough, chewy and difficult to digest.

**Serves 4**

10ml/2 tsp salt

10ml/2 tsp sugar

5ml/1 tsp coriander seeds,
crushed

3 allspice berries, lightly bruised

5ml/1 tsp dried chilli flakes

5ml/1 tsp chopped fresh dill

500g/1¼lb rainbow trout fillets,
skin on

90ml/6 tbsp rooibos tea leaves

baby salad leaves, to serve

**For the lime pickle**

10 limes

15ml/1 tbsp cardamom pods,
lightly bruised

15ml/1 tbsp nigella seeds

15ml/1 tbsp coriander seeds,
lightly crushed

20ml/4 tsp ground chillies

5ml/1 tsp ground turmeric

100ml/3½fl oz/scant ½ cup
vegetable oil

30ml/2 tbsp lime juice

**1** To make the lime pickle, cut the limes in half lengthways and cut away the central white pith from each section with a sharp knife, then cut each half in half again. Put the limes on a wire rack on a baking sheet, and bake in a low oven at 110°C/225°F/Gas ¼ for 1 hour. In the summer, if the weather is hot and dry, they can be dried on a rack in the sunshine until the skin is hardening.

**2** Dry-fry all the spices for the pickle in a medium pan over a low heat for 2 minutes, stirring. Add the oil and lime juice to the pan and warm through. Pack the dried limes into a clean and sterilized jar. Pour the spice mix over. Seal and store in a cool, dark place for about 3 weeks to mature.

**3** To cure the fish, combine the salt, sugar, coriander, allspice berries, chilli flakes and chopped dill in a small bowl. Sprinkle this mixture on to a medium baking tray or a large dinner plate.

**4** Place the fish fillets, skin side up, on to the salt and sugar mixture. Press the flesh side into the cure mix, then turn over so the fillets are skin side down. Leave for 2–3 hours in the refrigerator. When the fish has had its cure, wash off the mixture under cold running water. Pat dry with kitchen paper.

**5** Cut out a circle of foil about 10cm/4½in in diameter, then fashion it into a shallow bowl shape. Place in the bottom of a smoking box, potjie, or casserole pan and fill it with the tea leaves.

**6** Place a small bowl beside the foil bowl and fill this with ice. Place the fish fillets, skin side up, on a rack that will fit inside the smoker. Light the tea leaves with a blow torch, and when smoking place the rack holding the fish on top. Cover and leave to smoke for 30 minutes. If it is a particularly hot day place the smoker somewhere cool. Remove the lid and replace the ice and add some more tea leaves, light, cover, and repeat the smoking process again.

**7** Remove the fish from the smoker, cool then chill for 4 hours. Use a sharp knife to carve into very thin slices and serve with leaf salad and a little lime pickle. The fish will keep in the refrigerator for up to 3 days.

The Drakensberg mountains form the south eastern spine of South Africa, stretching across KwaZulu-Natal and into Lesotho.

# MEAT, POULTRY AND GAME …

*... There has always been an abundance of meat in South Africa, both hunted and herded.*

Beef is plentiful in South Africa and the lush green grasslands of the Natal midlands produce some of the finest in the whole of Africa, most famously used for biltong and boerewors. Ostrich meat is also popular, and is often used instead of beef in potjies and casseroles. Karoo lamb is world-renowned for its delicious herb-flavoured flesh, while chicken is regularly doused with spicy sauces, rubs and marinades before being roasted or grilled. Less universal dishes, which don't feature here, include township 'walkie talkies', a favourite dish made of chicken feet, head, hearts and intestine, or mopane worm stew.

# LAMB BOBOTIE

**Serves 6**

3 slices of day-old white bread, torn into small pieces

500ml/17fl oz/generous 2 cups full-fat (whole) milk

1kg/2¼lb/5 cups minced (ground) mutton or lamb shoulder

25ml/1½ tbsp ghee or virgin olive oil

3 red onions, finely chopped

4 cloves garlic, crushed

15ml/1 tbsp garam masala, plus extra for dusting

2.5ml/½ tsp ground turmeric

5ml/1 tsp ground cumin

5ml/1 tsp ground coriander

finely grated zest of 1 lemon

30ml/2 tbsp apricot jam (see page 148)

30ml/2 tbsp flaked (sliced) almonds

125g/4¼oz/½ cup sultanas (golden raisins)

butter, for greasing

4 eggs

1.5ml/¼ tsp freshly grated nutmeg

8–10 small bay leaves or lemon leaves

salt and black pepper

*Cook's tip* Mutton is *the traditional filling for bobotie, as it gives a greater depth of flavour, however lamb, or beef, will also do.*

*Traditionally served in little individual dishes ...*

This delightful dish, which was brought to South Africa by the Cape Malays, has added influences from the southern Mediterranean with its curd-like custard topping that is reminiscent of Greek moussaka. Boboties are traditionally made from meat that has been infused with spices and sweetened with dried fruit and apricot jam. Serve with some fragrant rice, mango atjar and cucumber sambal.

**1** Preheat the oven to 180°C/350°F/Gas 4. Soak the bread in 150ml/¼ pint/⅔ cup of the milk for 20 minutes. Squeeze the bread with your hand, discarding the excess milk. Mix the mutton with the soaked bread and season well with salt and pepper.

**2** Heat the ghee or oil in a medium-sized casserole or pan. Add the chopped onions and cook gently until for 8–10 minutes until soft and sweet, then add the garlic and cook for another couple of minutes.

**3** Stir the garam masala, turmeric, cumin, coriander and lemon zest into the onions, and cook for a further 2–3 minutes until the spices start to give off their aroma. Add the jam, almonds and sultanas. Remove the pan from the heat and stir in the meat and milk mixture.

**4** Grease 6 individual casseroles or ramekins with a little butter, and dust with some garam masala if you wish. Divide the meat mixture between the casseroles and then place on a baking sheet in the middle of the oven for 25–30 minutes.

**5** In another bowl, mix the eggs and the remaining milk and grated nutmeg. Season with salt and pepper. Remove the baking tray from the oven, top each dish with a bay leaf, and pour the milk mixture into the dishes to cover the partially-cooked meat mixture. Return to the oven and bake for a further 20 minutes until the tops have set and are light and golden. Serve hot with cucumber sambal.

*Cucumber sambal Peel, deseed and grate a small cucumber. Cut 150g/5oz cherry tomatoes in half and combine in a bowl with a handful each of chopped fresh mint and coriander (cilantro) leaves, and a finely chopped red chilli. Mix 45ml/3 tbsp white wine vinegar with 5ml/1 tsp sugar, then add to the bowl and mix through, adding salt and pepper to taste. Allow to stand for 15 minutes before serving.*

# TOMATO BREDIE WITH AMASI RAITA

**Serves 6–8**

30ml/2 tbsp ghee

1kg/2¼lb boned and trimmed lamb shoulder, cut into 5cm/2in chunks

5 red onions, peeled and sliced

4 cloves garlic, crushed

5cm/1in piece fresh root ginger, peeled and grated

3 small red chillies, chopped

5 allspice berries, lightly crushed

1 cinnamon stick, snapped in half

15ml/1 tbsp garam masala

2 bay leaves

500ml/17fl oz/generous 2 cups fresh chicken or lamb stock

1kg/2¼lb vine-ripened tomatoes, skinned, seeded and chopped

15ml/1 tbsp chopped fresh marjoram, plus leaves to garnish

15ml/1 tbsp brown sugar

10 small, waxy potatoes

steamed jasmine rice and quince sambal (see page 119), to serve

**For the amasi raita**

200ml/7fl oz/scant 1 cup amasi or natural (plain) yogurt

500g/1¼lb medium cucumber, peeled, seeded and grated

30ml/2 tbsp roughly chopped fresh mint

*Cook's tip* Amasi is the Zulu and Xhosa name for fermented milk, which is very popular in South Africa. It is believed to give strength, vitality and virility and it is said that the great Madiba wrote to his wife Winnie from Robben Island prison saying he had a great longing for it. A good quality natural (plain) yogurt can be used instead.

Bredie is a rich kind of stew, and is a familiar sight on the Cape Malay table. It is usually made with lamb, gently simmered with vegetables and spices, and traditionally would have been cooked in a large pan over an open fire. Tomatoes are added half way through the cooking, which slowly thicken the bredie to make a deliciously rich finished dish. The raita here is made with South Africa's much-loved fermented milk, amasi.

**1** Heat a large pan with a tight-fitting lid over a high heat. Add the ghee and the pieces of lamb and brown the meat all over. Transfer from the pan to a plate and set aside.

**2** Add the onions to the pan and cook over a medium heat until softened. Add the garlic, ginger, chillies, allspice berries, cinnamon stick, garam masala and bay leaves and cook for a further 1–2 minutes. Return the lamb to the pan and pour in the stock, scraping the bottom of the pan to remove any sediment that has accumulated.

**3** Bring the stock slowly to the simmer, cover, and cook on a very low heat for 1½ hours until the lamb is nearly tender.

**4** Add the chopped tomatoes, marjoram, sugar and potatoes to the pan and simmer for a further 40–45 minutes until the bredie has thickened and the potatoes are tender but not falling apart.

**5** To make the raita place the amasi, grated cucumber and mint in a small bowl and stir to mix. Serve the bredie with steamed rice, quince sambal, the raita and a little extra marjoram.

# SAMOOSAS

These are great South African favourites, the perfect snack eaten hot or cold, and believed to have been brought to the country by the Cape Malays, although samoosas, or one of the many derivatives, may have originally come from North Africa or the Middle East. They are traditionally stuffed with lamb or vegetables, and here they are served with a cool mango lassi to complement the fiery heat.

**Serves 8**

30ml/2 tbsp groundnut (peanut) oil, plus extra for deep-frying

1 large onion, finely chopped

200g/7oz/scant 1 cup lean minced (ground) lamb

5ml/1 tsp ground cumin

5ml/1 tsp ground coriander

generous pinch ground turmeric

10ml/2 tsp garam masala

1 clove garlic, crushed

3 large green chillies, deseeded and finely chopped

8 curry leaves

30ml/2 tbsp chopped fresh coriander (cilantro)

115g/4oz/1 cup peas

3 spring onions (scallions), finely sliced

45ml/3 tbsp flour

12 sheets pur or filo pastry, cut into 30cm x 7.5cm (12in x 3in) strips

salt and black pepper

blatjang (see page 110) or sweet chilli sauce, and lemon wedges, to serve

**For the mango lassi**

75ml/5 tbsp blended fresh mango, or canned mango pulp

150ml/¼ pint/⅔ cup natural (plain) yogurt

salt

**1** To make the samoosa filling, heat the oil in a frying pan. Add the onion and cook until soft and translucent. Increase the heat and add the lamb. Cook for 5 minutes until golden brown, stirring well.

**2** Lower the heat, add the cumin, ground coriander, turmeric and garam masala to the pan, and cook, stirring, for 2 minutes to release the aromas. Add the garlic, chillies and curry leaves and cook for another minute. Mix the fresh coriander, peas and spring onions into the lamb mixture, season with salt and pepper, then remove from the heat and set aside to cool.

**3** When the filling is completely cold, assemble the samoosas. Place the flour in a small bowl and mix with 30ml/2 tbsp cold water to form a thin paste. Lay a pastry strip out on the work surface, keeping the rest covered with a clean and damp dish towel.

**4** Fold the left edge of the pastry strip across to form a small triangle, fold down across to form another triangle, and make a small pocket. Add 1–2 teaspoons of the filling to the pocket, seal the edges with a little of the flour paste and fold over. Seal the edge with a little flour paste. Repeat to make 8–12 samoosas. Set aside in the refrigerator for 15–20 minutes to firm up until ready to fry.

**5** Prepare the lassi by mixing the mango pulp with the yogurt in a large jug (pitcher), and thin with enough cold water to make a pouring consistency; add a pinch of salt if desired. Chill in the refrigerator until ready to serve.

**6** Preheat the deep-fat fryer or a pan half filled with oil, to 180°C/350°F. Using a slotted spoon, carefully lower the samoosas into the oil, in batches of 3 or 4, and cook, turning frequently, for about 4 minutes until golden brown. Remove with a spoon and drain on crumpled kitchen paper.

**7** Serve the samoosas warm with blatjang or sweet chilli sauce and lemon wedges, accompanied by a glass of cold mango lassi.

Men and women who worked on the sugar plantations would stop off at backstreet cafes on the outskirts of Durban on their way to the fields to buy a bunny chow for their lunch.

# BUNNY CHOW WITH CORIANDER CHUTNEY

This worker's lunch comes from the Indian community in Durban and was invented in the 1940s as a meal that could be carried out to the sugar fields. A bunny is basically a helping of spicy stew served in a hollowed-out loaf, with the scooped-out bread placed on top like a little hat to avoid spillages. Shoulder of lamb or mutton is perfect for this slow-cooked recipe, as it has good amounts of fat to give flavour and tenderness. A bunny should be fairly fiery, and here it is served with a tangy coriander chutney.

**Serves 4**

30ml/2 tbsp groundnut (peanut) oil
500g/1¼lb lamb shoulder, boned, and cut into 2cm/1in cubes
2 red onions, peeled and finely chopped
3 cloves garlic, peeled and crushed
5cm/2½in piece fresh root ginger, grated
2 small red chillies, deseeded and finely chopped
5ml/1 tsp cumin seeds
5ml/1 tsp fennel seeds
1 cinnamon stick
3 cardamom pods, lightly bruised
2 bay leaves
12 curry leaves
15ml/1 tbsp garam masala
3 large tomatoes
500ml/⅔ pint/2 cups fresh lamb or chicken stock
2 large potatoes, peeled and diced
salt and black pepper
2 small loaves white bread

**For the coriander chutney**
115g/4oz bunch fresh coriander (cilantro)
1 green chilli, deseeded and finely chopped
5ml/1 tsp grated fresh root ginger
1 clove garlic, crushed
30ml/2 tbsp groundnut (peanut) oil
5ml/1 tsp ground cumin
15ml/1 tbsp lemon juice

**1** Heat the oil in a large pan over a medium heat. Brown the meat on all sides, remove from the pan and set aside.

**2** Cook the onions in the pan for 5–6 minutes until soft but not coloured, add the garlic, grated ginger and chillies and cook for another 2–3 minutes. Add the cumin and fennel seeds and cook for about 2 minutes until the aromas are released, then stir in the cinnamon stick, cardamom, bay leaves, curry leaves and garam masala.

**3** Place the tomatoes in just-boiled water to loosen the skins, then peel and chop the flesh. Add the tomatoes to the spiced onions, and cook until they soften a little.

**4** Return the browned meat to the spiced onions mixture, add the stock and cover. Simmer for about 35–40 minutes. Add the diced potatoes and continue to cook for a further 15–20 minutes until the potatoes are tender. Season with a little salt and pepper to taste.

**5** Meanwhile make the coriander chutney: place all the ingredients in a blender or food processor and blend to a smooth consistency. Add salt and pepper to taste, then pour into a clean small glass jar and seal. This can be kept in the refrigerator for up to 5 days.

**6** To serve the bunny chow, cut the loaves in half and hollow out the insides of each section, reserving the bread that is scooped out. Ladle the warm curry into the loaf cavities, spoon a little coriander chutney on top and cover with the reserved bread; wrap in paper if it's to be transported, or eat at once.

*Portable and filling food, designed to make a little go a long way ...*

# CHICKEN AND PRAWN CURRY

**Serves 4**

This dish has echoes of the Malabar Coast some 4,000 miles away, where curries are prepared by Keralan cooks using coconut milk bases and warm spices. Indian migrants arrived in South Africa from this area 100 years ago to work on the sugar cane fields along the sub-tropical east coast. This curry, served with cooling coriander and yellow rice, adds prawns to the chicken, together with fresh mango and coconut.

### For the curry

30ml/2 tbsp groundnut (peanut) oil

2 red onions, finely chopped

4 cloves garlic, peeled and crushed

5cm/2in piece fresh root ginger, peeled and grated

3 red chillies, finely chopped

2.5ml/½ tsp turmeric

30ml/2 tbsp medium curry powder

small bunch curry leaves, about 12

3 large vine-ripened tomatoes, peeled, seeded and chopped

350g/12oz skinless chicken breast fillets, sliced into 2cm/1in strips

12 large unpeeled prawns (jumbo shrimp), deveined

400ml/14fl oz/1⅔ cups cups coconut milk

45ml/3 tbsp chopped fresh coriander (cilantro)

salt and black pepper

### For the yellow rice

200g/7oz/1 cup jasmine rice

pinch of saffron

4 cardamom pods, lightly bruised

1 cinnamon stick, snapped in half

50g/2oz/½ cup cashew nuts, toasted

**1** Heat the oil in a medium pan, add the onions and cook for 5 minutes until soft and translucent. Add the garlic, ginger and chillies and cook for a further 2 minutes.

**2** Add the turmeric and curry powder to the pan and cook for a further one minute. Add the curry leaves, chopped tomatoes and chicken. Cook for 3 minutes, stirring, until the chicken has changed colour and is almost cooked through. Add the prawns and stir gently, then pour in the coconut milk, stirring to remove any residue or spices that are stuck to the bottom of the pan. Simmer for 6–8 minutes, until the sauce has slightly thickened and the prawns are bright pink. Remove from the heat and keep warm.

**3** Rinse the rice well under cold running water. Add the rice to a pan with a tightly-fitting lid, together with 400ml/14fl oz/1⅔ cups cold water, the saffron, cardamom pods and cinnamon stick. Bring to the boil, cover, and simmer gently for 10 minutes until all the water has been absorbed. Remove the lid and place a clean dish towel over the rice and set aside for 10 minutes. Add the toasted cashew nuts and fluff with a fork.

**4** Stir the fresh coriander into the curry, check for seasoning, adding a little more salt and pepper if needed, and serve in warmed bowls with the rice.

# KUDU PIE

The kudu is a member of the antelope family. It is a large beast, much larger than the more common springbok. Use meat from the haunch of the animal rather than the loin, as the working muscle makes it ideal for cooking slowly. A little fatty bacon will also help with the flavour and tenderness of the meat. The recipe uses a rough puff pastry, which is a good halfway point between shortcrust and puffed pastry. Ensure that the butter for the pastry is well chilled.

**Serves 4**

30ml/2 tbsp vegetable oil

25g/1 oz butter

1kg/2¼lb kudu haunch, cut into bitesize pieces

150g/5oz streaky (fatty) bacon, diced

2 onions, peeled and sliced

4 medium carrots, peeled and sliced

4 sticks celery

2 bay leaves

3 cloves garlic, crushed

3 cloves

1.5ml/¼ tsp finely grated nutmeg

4 allspice berries

4 juniper berries

30ml/2 tbsp plain (all-purpose) flour

300ml/½ pint/1¼ cups pale ale or light beer

125ml/4fl oz/½ cup apricot jam (see page 148)

beer bread (see page 138), to serve

**For the pastry**

300g/11oz/2 cups strong white flour

a pinch fine sea salt

300g/10oz chilled butter, cubed

150ml/¼ pint/⅔ cup cold water

1 beaten egg, for glazing

**1** Preheat the oven to 140°C/275°F/Gas 1. Heat the oil in a large casserole over a medium heat. When oil is hot add the butter and allow to bubble before adding the meat. Cook until the meat is browned all over. Remove with a slotted spoon and set aside. Add the bacon, onions, carrots and celery and cook for 10 minutes until the vegetables have softened.

**2** Return the meat to the pan, add the bay leaves, garlic, cloves, nutmeg and berries and cook for 1 minute. Sprinkle in the flour and stir until the meat and vegetables are coated with it. Add the pale ale, scrape any residue from the bottom of the pan and stir in the apricot jam. Bring to a simmer, then cover and place in the oven for 50 minutes to an hour until the meat is tender but not falling apart. Allow to cool before use.

**3** Make the pastry by sifting the flour and salt into a medium mixing bowl. Add the butter and cut into the flour with a knife until you have small lumps coated in flour. Make a well in the middle and slowly add the water, mixing it together until you have a firm dough. Place in clear film (plastic wrap) and allow to rest in the refrigerator for 30 minutes.

**4** Knead the chilled pastry on a lightly floured surface. Roll in one direction to make a large rectangle about 25cm x 50cm/10 x 20in. Fold the top third section of pastry down to the middle and then fold the bottom third over the top. Turn the dough by a quarter, and roll gently and neatly again to 3 times its length. Repeat the folding, the turn and roll again. Repeat the folding, turning and rolling twice more, then cover in clear film, and chill until ready to use.

**5** Place the pie mixture into 4 individual pie dishes, or 1 2 litre/3½ pint dish, filling to just below the rim. On a lightly floured surface roll the pastry and cut 4 rounds large enough to top the dishes with a 2cm/¾in overhang. Trim and press around the edges to seal. Brush the surface of the pastry with the beaten egg. Cut a small slit in the middle of the pies. Place in the refrigerator for 20 minutes. Preheat the oven to 180°C/350°F/Gas 4.

**6** Brush a little more glaze on to the surface of the pies, then bake in the oven for 25–30 minutes until crisp and golden. Serve the pies hot, with beer bread to mop up the juices.

Some say that Boer trekkers discovered biltong by accident
when they placed pieces of meat under the saddle of their
horses, which was warmed, dried and flattened as they rode.

# GAME BILTONG

Today this is South Africa's most famous snack, served everywhere from gourmet restaurants to filling stations. Game would have been the voortrekkers only available source of fresh meat, and biltong was a speedy way of making the most of a successful hunt as they trekked north and east into the interior of the country. Some cuts would have been eaten almost immediately, while rumps and loins would be cured for times when meat was scarce.

**Makes about 1kg/2lb**

60ml/4 tbsp coriander seeds

10ml/2 tsp black peppercorns

5ml/1 tsp ground cloves

30ml/2 tbsp chilli flakes

60ml/4 tbsp sea salt flakes

75ml/2½fl oz/⅓ cup red wine vinegar

25ml/1½ tbsp Worcestershire sauce

2kg/4½lb springbok or kudu loin, trimmed and cut into 4 equal-width sections

2.5ml/½ tsp bicarbonate of soda (baking soda)

pickled cucumbers, bread and butter and quince jam (see page 146), to serve

**1** In a dry frying pan place the coriander and peppercorns and toast for a minute or two until the aromas are released. Crush them coarsely in a pestle and mortar. Add the cloves, chilli flakes and salt to the spices, and mix.

**2** Pour the vinegar and Worcestershire sauce into a shallow dish and add the meat, turning to coat. Add the spice mix with the bicarbonate of soda and turn the meat over and over, pressing it into the spice mixture to make sure all the meat is covered with the spice mix.

**3** Cover the dish with clear film (plastic wrap) and place in the refrigerator for at least 12 hours. Turn the meat in the mixture every 4 hours, pressing the crushed spices into the meat.

**4** Remove the meat from the dish. Use a trussing needle to make a hole through the meat about 4cm/2in from the end of each strip. Tie a small knot on the end of a piece of string about 15cm/7in long and thread the string through the hole. Tie the knot so the meat is now ready to hang in a biltong maker, available online, or outside.

**5** Hanging the meat will depend on the time of year. In the summer months the meat will dry quickly, in winter it will take longer. In hot weather hang the meat on a pole near an open window. Place a small fan below the meat to keep the air moving and deter insects. Leave for around 5 days depending on how moist you prefer it. When the biltong is to your liking, whether moist or slightly dry, wrap in baking parchment.

**6** Serve the biltong thinly sliced, accompanied with plenty of pickled cucumbers, bread and butter and quince jam. Keep wrapped in the refrigerator and consume within a week.

*Cook's tip* We used springbok for this recipe, an animal that is synonymous with South Africa. Its meat is tasty, lean and it is widely available from specialist shops or online.

# BEEF BILTONG

Once the trekkers settled down they continued to preserve meat in the same way, still with game, but also with farm-bred animals. Old Dutch-style farmhouses were built in stone and had thatched roofs, and internal temperature levels could be closely controlled. Food was dried in the eaves, while flag-stoned floors and deep wall cavities were perfect for cool storage. Biltong and droëwors (cured sausages) were hung in a cupboard above the chimney where a consistent warm temperature was ideal for drying.

**Makes about 1kg/2lb**

2kg/4½lb piece of rump or
silverside beef, trimmed
45ml/3 tbsp coriander seeds
30ml/2 tbsp mixed peppercorns
6 allspice berries
60ml/4 tbsp dark brown soft sugar
40g/1½oz fine sea salt
10ml/2 tsp Worcestershire sauce
60ml/4 tbsp brown malt vinegar
5ml/1 tsp bicarbonate of soda
(baking soda)

**1** Place the meat in the freezer for 2–3 hours. When the meat is stiff cut it into 3–4cm/1½–2in-thick oval sections, or fillets, cutting down the grain of the meat. If the meat is still frozen, allow it to defrost. Using a trussing needle make a small hole in the top of each fillet.

**2** Warm a medium-sized frying pan over a low heat. Add the coriander seeds, mixed peppercorns and allspice berries and toast for 2–3 minutes until the aroma of the spices is released and the pieces have been lightly toasted. Grind in a pestle and mortar until the spices are rough but not too fine then transfer to a medium-sized bowl.

**3** Add the salt and sugar to the bowl and mix well. Spread the spice mixture all over the pieces of meat, pressing it into the flesh. Combine the Worcestershire sauce and the vinegar together, stir in the bicarbonate of soda and pour the fizzing mixture over the meat. Leave the beef to cure in an airtight container for 24 hours, turning the meat over every 6 hours.

**4** When the meat has cured, discard the liquid that has been released. Take each piece of beef, thread some butcher's twine through the hole in the top and secure with a knot.

**5** Hang the meat on a small rail and place in a warm dry place that has some ventilation. Place a drip tray underneath and position a small fan to help circulate the air and keep insects away. Leave for about 1–2 weeks. You could also hang the beef in a dehydrator or biltong maker; this will speed up the process, taking around 48 hours.

**6** The meat will lose almost half of its weight during this process and will be semi-dried, giving a pink colour and chewy texture. Hang for a few more days if you prefer it firmer or want it to last longer. Once it is dried to your liking, wrap the biltong in baking parchment and chill for up to a week, or freeze for up to 3 months.

**7** Slice the biltong as thin as you can and serve as a tasty snack with ice-cold beer, buttered bread, some blatjang (see page 110) and some pickled gherkins, or have it as an African trail mix, mixing it with chopped dried prunes, almonds, apricots and pumpkin seeds.

# SPRINGBOK CARPACCIO

This is a South African twist on the classic Italian dish carpaccio; very thinly sliced raw meat or fish served with a tangy sauce. In this recipe the meat is quickly seared on the braai and flavoured with herbs and rooibos tea, which helps to tenderize the meat. Chill the meat in the freezer for about half an hour before serving so you can carve wafer-thin slices.

**Serves 4**

200g/7oz springbok loin
10ml/2 tsp coriander seeds
15ml/1 tbsp rooibos tea leaves
10ml/2 tsp finely chopped fresh rosemary leaves
5ml/1 tsp finely chopped fresh thyme leaves
olive oil, for drizzling
salt and black pepper
a few handfuls fresh pea shoots or rocket (arugula), to serve

**For the dressing**
75ml/2½fl oz/⅓ cup olive oil
zest and juice of 1 lemon
7.5ml/1½ tsp chopped capers

**1** To prepare the springbok loin, trim off all the excess fat and sinew. Roll the meat into a cylindrical shape by tying butcher's string at equal intervals down its length and knotting tightly. Dry well by blotting with kitchen paper. Prepare the braai.

**2** Lightly toast the coriander seeds in a dry frying pan, then crush roughly in a pestle and mortar. Transfer to a baking tray, adding and mixing in the tea and herbs. Take the springbok and roll it over in the seed mixture, pushing gently so that the coating sticks to the outside of the meat. Drizzle 30ml/2 tbsp oil all over the meat.

**3** When the flames on the braai have died down, quickly sear the springbok on all sides until golden. Remove, set aside to cool, then place in the freezer for half an hour to firm up until ready to serve.

**4** Meanwhile prepare the dressing by mixing the olive oil, lemon zest and juice and chopped capers in a bowl, adding a little salt and pepper to taste.

**5** To serve, use a very sharp knife to cut the meat into wafer-thin slices. Arrange a few slices on each plate. Season with a little salt and pepper. Drizzle a small amount of the dressing over the meat. Dress the pea shoots with some of the dressing, and place on the plate. Keep any leftover carpaccio for up to 5 days, in the refrigerator, wrapped in baking parchment.

*Carpaccio makes an excellent appetizer for a dinner party...*

# ACCOMPANIMENTS AND SIDE DISHES ...

*... When the first Dutch settlers arrived in the Cape they foraged on wild sorrel and asparagus growing up the slopes of Table Mountain.*

The first successfully cultivated fresh vegetables of the Cape were lettuces and radishes, which could grow quickly in the warm sun, but the Dutch settlers soon introduced pumpkins, gourds, cucumbers and sweet potatoes as well as vine and citrus fruits. The Malays then brought aromatic rice dishes, dhals, pumpkin bredies, crunchy hot sambals and exotic date salads. The traditional African diet places more importance on the side dishes and starches than the meat or fish, possibly due to its availability and sustaining effects. Dishes such as setjesta, for example, a combination of mealie meal and pumpkin, is ideal on its own or for soaking up meat juices from the braai.

# ROASTED BUTTERNUT SQUASH SOUP

Butternut squash are grown in the Highveld, Lowveld and Gauteng provinces of South Africa throughout the summer, then harvested and stored to eat through the winter. Roasting the squash gives a greater intensity of flavour, and you could do this in a foil parcel on the braai. Toasted pumpkin seeds give a lovely crunch to the creamy soup.

**Serves 6**

3 red onions, peeled and quartered

500g/1¼lb/2¼ cups peeled and chopped butternut squash

30ml/2 tbsp olive oil

1 red chilli, deseeded and chopped

3 cloves garlic, crushed

2.5ml/½ tsp ground cumin

5ml/1 tsp ground coriander

2.5ml/½ tsp ground ginger

900ml/1½ pints/3¾ cups hot vegetable stock

1 small ripe mango, peeled and diced

salt and black pepper

45ml/3 tbsp toasted pumpkin seeds, chopped fresh coriander (cilantro), lime juice and natural (plain) yogurt, to serve

**1** Preheat the oven to 200°C/400°F/Gas 6. Place the onions and squash in a deep heavy roasting pan and drizzle with the olive oil. Season with a little salt to help crisp the edges. Roast for 15–20 minutes, until the vegetables are golden and tender.

**2** Remove the roasting pan from the oven and place on the top of the stove over a low heat. Add the chilli, garlic and spices and cook, stirring, for 2 minutes until the oil and spices have coated the vegetables.

**3** Add the stock to the roasting pan, stirring to remove any traces from the bottom, and transfer the contents into a medium-sized pan. Gently bring to the boil and simmer for 10 minutes until the vegetables are tender.

**4** Remove from the heat and add the diced mango. Blend with a stick blender or in a food processor until smooth. Ladle into bowls and serve with toasted pumpkin seeds, lots of chopped coriander, lime juice, black pepper, and a swirl of natural yogurt.

**Serves 8**

450g/1lb/4 cups mealie flour
(maize flour)

45ml/3 tbsp corn oil, plus extra
for frying

750ml/1¼ pints/3 cups vegetable
stock

275g/10oz/generous 1 cup minced
(ground) lamb

1 red onion, finely grated

3 cloves garlic, crushed

2 small red chillies, finely chopped

5cm/2in piece fresh root ginger,
finely grated

30ml/2 tbsp medium curry powder

3 medium vine-ripened tomatoes,
skinned, seeded and chopped

75g/3oz dried apricots, finely chopped

75g/3oz dried mango, finely chopped

30ml/2 tbsp chopped fresh
coriander (cilantro)

45ml/3 tbsp flour, for dusting

salt and black pepper

lemon wedges, to serve

**For the ketchup**

1 medium ripe pineapple,
peeled, cored and sliced

1 large ripe mango, peeled, stone (pit)
removed and roughly chopped

90g/3½oz/½ cup white sugar

150ml/¼ pint/⅔ cup white
wine vinegar

30ml/1 tbsp lime juice

2 red chillies, finely chopped

# MEALIE CROQUETTES

These delicious, crispy balls made with maize flour make a great snack or appetizer to enjoy with a cold beer after a day in the hot sun. Serve with some spicy pineapple ketchup.

**1** To make the ketchup, place the pineapple, mango, sugar and vinegar into a pan and cook over a medium heat until the fruits are tender. Strain, reserving the liquid, and blend the fruit to a smooth purée, adding a little reserved liquid and lime juice to give a ketchup-like consistency. Stir in the chopped chillies and decant into a clean bottle or bowl until ready to serve.

**2** Mix the mealie flour with 30ml/2 tbsp corn oil in a large pan. Add the stock and cook over a medium heat, stirring, until thickened. Season well with salt and pepper and set aside.

**3** Heat the remaining 15ml/1 tbsp oil in a large frying pan over a medium heat. Add the lamb and cook, stirring and separating the meat, until golden. Add the onion and cook until softened, add the garlic, chillies and ginger and cook for another couple of minutes.

**4** Add the curry powder to the lamb mixture and cook for a further minute. Add the chopped tomatoes and cook for about 8–10 minutes until soft and pulpy. Remove from the heat, stir in the apricots, mango, and the coriander and leave to cool.

**5** Stir the cooled lamb into the mealie mixture, then shape into small balls. Set aside in the refrigerator to firm up a little.

**6** Heat the corn oil in a pan or a deep fat fryer to 180°C/350°F. Dust the balls in a little flour, then lower them a few at a time into the hot oil. Cook until crispy and golden. Drain on kitchen paper and season with a little more salt. Serve hot with the pineapple and mango ketchup and lemon wedges.

Maize, or corn, is known as mealies in South Africa.
The crop was introduced by the Portuguese, who called
it 'milho.'

# MEALIE CURRY WITH PARATHAS

**Serves 4**

6 corn cobs, husks removed
30ml/2 tbsp vegetable oil
2 red onions, peeled and finely chopped
30ml/2 tbsp black mustard seeds
12 curry leaves
400ml/14fl oz/1⅔ cups coconut milk
30ml/2 tbsp desiccated (dry unsweetened shredded) coconut
sweet chill sauce, to serve

**For the curry paste**
150g/5oz fresh coriander (cilantro), stems trimmed, plus extra, chopped, to serve
4 medium green chillies, deseeded and roughly chopped
5cm/2in piece fresh root ginger, peeled and grated
4 cloves garlic, roughly chopped

**For the parathas**
350g/12oz plain (all-purpose) flour
5ml/1 tsp fine salt
30ml/2 tbsp vegetable oil
250g/9oz butter, softened
groundnut (peanut) oil, for frying
salt and black pepper

This simple curry is enriched with cooling coconut milk that takes the heat out of the chillies. It can be served as a side dish to accompany plain grilled fish, or as a main course served with the delicious crispy flatbreads.

**1** To make the curry paste, place the coriander, chillies, ginger and garlic in a small food processor. Pulse until smooth. Transfer to an airtight container and chill until required.

**2** Chop the corn into 2cm/1in sections. Cook in salted boiling water for 4 minutes, drain and set aside. Heat the oil in a medium pan, add the onions and cook for 5 minutes until soft but not coloured. Add the mustard seeds and stir until they start to pop. Add the curry paste and cook for 2 minutes until the aromas are released, then add the curry leaves, coconut milk, desiccated coconut and the corn sections. Cover and simmer gently for 6 minutes.

**3** To make the parathas, place the flour and salt in a large mixing bowl. Add the oil; use the tips of your fingers to rub the oil into to the flour. Gradually add about 200ml/7fl oz/scant 1 cup of water to make a soft and sticky dough.

**4** Tip the dough on to a lightly floured surface. Roll out to a large rectangle about 35 x 20cm/14 x 8in. Spread the softened butter evenly over the surface. Roll up tightly like a Swiss (jelly) roll. Place in the refrigerator to firm up and rest for about 30 minutes. Slice the dough across into 2cm/1in pieces. Use a rolling pin to roll each into a small disc, about 25cm/10in diameter. Return to the refrigerator or freezer for about 20 minutes to firm up.

**5** Heat 5ml/1 tsp oil in a large frying pan on a medium heat, and fry the parathas for about 2 minutes until crisp and golden, then flip over and cook the other side. Remove and drain on kitchen paper, set aside and keep warm. Serve the mealie curry with the parathas and some sweet chilli sauce.

Serve the curry garnished with chopped
coriander and accompanied by the warm parathas.

# SETJESTA

This very simple dish, a little like smooth polenta, has its origins in the Freestate, but is eaten nationwide. It is made with mealie meal (ground maize) or 'pap', mixed with pumpkin or butternut squash. Portuguese traders introduced mealie pap to Africa from its colonies in South America, and it quickly became a great staple of the whole African continent. The finished texture of pap can vary from soft and moist to dry and crumbly.

**Serves 4**

1 butternut squash or small pumpkin, about 1kg/2¼lb
165g/5½oz/1¼ cups mealie meal
75g/3oz/6 tbsp butter
500ml/17fl oz/generous 2 cups full-fat (whole) milk
30ml/2tbsp corn oil
1 medium red onion, finely sliced
salt and black pepper
butter, to serve

*Cook's tip* Setjesta is an excellent accompaniment to roasted meat or fish.

**1** Preheat the oven to 180°C/350°F/Gas 4. Wash the squash and pat dry. Place on a baking sheet and roast for 40–45 minutes until the skin is soft and slightly golden. Remove and set aside to cool.

**2** Place the mealie meal, butter and milk in a medium pan and bring to a gentle simmer. Simmer for about 15 minutes until the meal is cooked. Remove and set aside.

**3** Heat the oil in a heavy frying pan. Add the sliced onion and cook over a medium heat until soft and slightly golden.

**4** Take the cooled squash and cut it in half. Remove and discard the seeds and fibre, then scoop the soft flesh from the outer skin into a bowl. Stir in plenty of salt and pepper and the cooked onions.

**5** Add the squash and onion mixture to the mealie meal, stir well and serve as soon as possible with a little more salt, pepper and butter.

# BLATJANG

Blatjang is best described as a cross between a runny chutney and a jam, and its unique sweet, sour and spicy flavour packs a fiery punch. It was brought to South Africa by the Javanese and is the traditional accompaniment to bobotie. We took advantage of the hot South African sun to dry our own fresh apricots and peaches, but you can also, of course, use commerically dried fruit.

**Makes approx 3kg/6½lb**

225g/8oz/1 cup semi-dried apricots

225g/8oz/1 cup semi-dried peaches

450g/1lb/2½ cups sultanas (golden raisins)

500ml/17fl oz/generous 2 cups white wine vinegar

6 red onions, peeled

cloves from 1 large head of garlic, finely crushed

500g/1¼lb/2½ cups dark, soft brown sugar

400g/4oz/2 cups blanched almonds

60ml/4 tbsp sea salt flakes

5cm/2in piece fresh ginger, grated

30ml/2 tbsp coriander seeds, toasted and lightly ground

30ml/2 tbsp brown mustard seeds, toasted and lightly crushed

3 fresh red chillies, finely chopped

2 bay leaves

**1** Soak the apricots, peaches and sultanas in the vinegar overnight. To speed up this process, either bring the vinegar to the boil and pour it over the dried fruits or leave the soaking fruits out in a warm place.

**2** The following day preheat the oven to 180°C/350°F/Gas 4. Place the peeled onions in a roasting pan and bake for 30–35 minutes until tender. Remove, set aside, and when cool enough to handle, chop finely.

**3** Prepare the jars by placing them in a dishwasher and setting on a high cycle. Or wash the jars and lids scrupulously in hot water and place the jars into a preheated oven at 110°C/225°F/Gas ¼ for 15 minutes.

**4** Place the soaked fruits, with the vinegar, into a large wide pan about 5 litres/9 pints in volume, or a pressure cooker is ideal. Add the chopped onion and the rest of the ingredients, and stir to combine. Cook over a medium heat, stirring, for about 20–25 minutes until the mixture is a deep amber colour, and has reduced to a thick, jam-like consistency. Remove the pan from the heat, discard the bay leaves, and blend with a hand blender.

**5** When the blatjang is still hot, pour the mixture into the sterilized jars and seal with lids. Store in a cool, dry, dark cupboard for at least a month, and up to 1 year. Once open keep in the refrigerator for up to 3 weeks.

# PICKLED **ACHARD**

This is a great little accompaniment, rather like a crunchy coleslaw, that originates in Mauritius but has been adopted by the Cape Malays. It is ideal for a picnic, as the salad can be dressed a few hours before serving to help develop the flavours, but shouldn't sit too long otherwise the crunch of the nuts and vegetables will be lost. A food processor with a grating attachment would make this a really quick dish to put together, otherwise you'll need a sharp, heavy knife and a large chopping board.

**Serve 4–6**

½ hard, white cabbage, finely shredded
6 large carrots, peeled and grated
100g/3¾oz sugar snap peas, sliced lengthways
3 spring onions (scallions), thinly sliced
115g/4oz/1 cup cashew nuts, lightly toasted and finely chopped
45ml/3 tbsp chopped fresh coriander (cilantro)
2 small red chillies, finely chopped
5cm/2in piece ginger, finely grated
3 cloves garlic, crushed

**For the dressing**
100ml/3½fl oz/scant ½ cup groundnut (peanut) oil
45ml/3 tbsp white wine vinegar
5ml/1 tsp garam masala
5ml/1 tsp mustard seeds
1 pinch sugar
juice of 1 lime
salt and black pepper

**1** Once you have shredded, peeled, grated, chopped and sliced all the ingredients, place them together in a large mixing bowl and mix with your hands to combine.

**2** Mix all the dressing ingredients together in a small pan or bowl and season with salt and pepper to taste. Pour the dressing over the vegetables and mix through until all the vegetables are evenly coated.

**3** Store, covered, or in an airtight container in the refrigerator for up to 2 hours until ready to serve. If you're eating later than this, store the salad without adding the dressing.

**4** To serve, toss the salad again and serve as an accompaniment to braais, pies, roast meats or grilled (broiled) fish.

# HERITAGE TOMATO CHUTNEY

This classic preserve deals with the end of summer glut of tomatoes, and it's fine to use under-ripe fruit as well as the knobbly imperfect ones you might find lingering on the vine. As it's a traditional South African recipe we used heritage tomatoes.

**Makes about 1.75 litres/
3 pints/7½ cups**

12 large vine-ripened tomatoes
2 large red (bell) peppers
45ml/3 tbsp chilli oil
500g/1¼lb red onions, finely chopped
15ml/1 tbsp mustard seeds
3 cloves garlic, crushed
3 red chillies, deseeded and chopped
2 bay leaves
1 branch curry leaves
1 large, ripe papaya, peeled, seeded
and chopped
200g/7oz/1 cup sugar
200ml/7fl oz/scant 1 cup red
wine vinegar
15ml/1 tbsp Worcestershire sauce
10ml/2 tsp soy sauce
salt and black pepper

**1** Sterilize your jars by placing in the dishwasher at the highest temperature and then place in the oven at 110°C/225°F/Gas ¼ for 15 minutes. Set aside and keep warm.

**2** Grill the tomatoes on the braai, or blanch in just-boiled water, remove the skins, discard the seeds, and chop the flesh.

**3** Cut the peppers in half, remove the seeds and then grill on the braai or roast in a hot oven until the skins begin to scorch. Remove from the heat, cover with a clean dish towel and when cool, peel off the skin. Chop the peppers into strips.

**4** Heat the oil over a medium heat in a large deep pan. Add the onions and cook gently for 10–15 minutes until soft and translucent, then add the mustard seeds and cook for 1 minute until they start to pop. Stir in the garlic, chillies, bay leaves and curry leaves and cook for 2 minutes until the aromas are released. Add the chopped tomatoes and roasted pepper strips and cook until the tomatoes are slightly pulpy.

**5** Add the papaya and cook for 1 minute. Stir in the sugar, red wine vinegar, Worcestershire sauce, soy sauce and seasoning to taste. Loosely cover and bring to a simmer over a medium heat. Cook on a low heat for 30–35 minutes until the mixture is thick and reduced. Pour into the warm jars and seal.

**6** Store in a cool, dark cupboard for at least a month to allow the flavours to develop, and for up to 6 months. Serve with crusty bread and cheese, and, once open, store in the refrigerator.

*Cook's tip* Cooking the tomatoes and peppers on the braai will give a mild smoky flavour, but you can also use a grill (broiler).

# MANGO AND PEACH ATJAR

Atjar is another delicious condiment introduced by the Malays, and often appears on the South African table when curry is being served. Although there is a wide variety of atjars available in the stores and supermarkets people often make their own when seasonal ingredients are plentiful, capturing that height-of-ripe flavour. As we travelled from the Western Cape to the east the recipes we found showed noticeable variations in the levels of spicy heat; this version lies somewhere in the middle.

**Makes 500ml/17fl oz/ 2 cups**

8 black peppercorns
3 allspice berries, lightly crushed
1 medium dried chilli
500g/1¼lb firm green mangoes, peeled, stoned (pitted) and chopped
500g/1¼lb ripe peaches, stoned (pitted) and chopped
75g/3oz/½ cup seedless raisins
2 red onions, finely chopped
50g/2oz/½ cup flaked (sliced) almonds, toasted
125ml/4fl oz/½ cup white wine vinegar
125g/4¼oz/generous ½ cup white sugar
5ml/1 tsp ground ginger
5ml/1 tsp turmeric
2 bay leaves
15ml/1 tbsp medium curry powder
poppadums, to serve

1 Sterilize your jars by placing in the dishwasher at the highest temperature and then place in the oven at 110°C/225°F/Gas ¼ for 15 minutes. Set aside and keep warm.

2 Tie the peppercorns, allspice and dried chilli into a small square of muslin (cheesecloth) and place in a medium pan. Add the rest of the ingredients, loosely cover and slowly bring to a simmer, stirring regularly to dissolve the sugar.

3 Turn up the heat and simmer for about 50 minutes until the sauce starts to thicken and the fruits are soft but not breaking down. Gently stir occasionally to prevent any sticking to the base of the pan. Check for seasoning then remove the muslin parcel and transfer the atjar into the warmed jars.

4 Store in a dark place for around 3 to 4 weeks. Serve with any type of curry, or as an accompaniment to poppadums, and once opened, store in the refrigerator.

*This wonderful sweet and sour pickle can also be eaten with bredies or bobotie.*

# SAMBALS

The first Malay cooks that arrived in the Western Cape had a great understanding of texture, flavour and the balance of food. Sambals are from Indonesia and Sri Lanka, and are little dishes of fruit and vegetables to accompany curries, adding tangy flavours and crunch to a meal. Sambals are best prepared at the last minute.

## BANANA SAMBAL

**Serves 4**

3 ripe bananas
juice of 2 limes
1 small red onion, finely chopped
2.5ml/½ tsp sugar
1 green chilli, deseeded and very finely chopped
30ml/2 tbsp fresh chopped coriander (cilantro)
6 baby cucumbers, diced
salt and black pepper

Serve this sharp, sweet sambal with a spiced vegetable curry; it is also great with the grilled fish on page 28.

**1** Peel and slice the banana, and toss gently with 30ml/2 tbsp lime juice in a bowl.

**2** Mix in the other ingredients, taste, and add seasoning and extra lime juice if needed. Transfer into small bowls and serve.

## QUINCE SAMBAL

**Serves 4**

1 large ripe quince
5ml/1 tsp salt
juice of 1 lemon
2 small bird's eye red chillies, deseeded and finely chopped
5ml/1 tsp sugar
1 small red onion, peeled and finely chopped

The quince harvest, which begins mid-March, is eagerly anticipated in South Africa; often the fruit is bottled or preserved as a kind of apple sauce, but this sambal makes use of the ripe fruit. It is very good served with grilled oily fish. Quinces need to be picked when they are yellow and lush; if they are under-ripe they are hard and sour. This sambal is excellent served with tomato bredie.

**1** Peel and core the quince. Grate into long elegant strips and sprinkle with salt.

**2** Place into a large bowl, add the rest of the ingredients and toss gently to combine. Allow to stand for 10 minutes before serving.

## PAPAYA SAMBAL

**Serves 4**

30ml/2 tbsp white wine vinegar
½ small cucumber, peeled, deseeded and sliced into long strips
30ml/2 tbsp fresh chopped coriander (cilantro)
½ small papaya and 1 small pineapple, peeled and chopped into chunks
1 small red chilli, deseeded and chopped
salt and black pepper

This sambal offers the sanctity of a cool place, and makes an ideal refuge from a fiery masala fish, or as a fruity bite with lamb sosaties.

**1** Place the vinegar in a medium-sized mixing bowl and add all the chopped ingredients. Season with a little salt and pepper.

**2** Transfer to small serving bowls and serve swiftly before the papaya becomes soft.

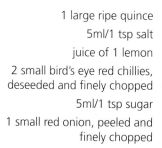

# BAKING, PRESERVES AND DRINKS ...

*... South Africans love to preserve and bottle, and multi-cultural influences have created a wonderful baking tradition.*

The Company Gardens established by Jan Van Riebeeck meant that bountiful harvests needed to be conserved, and the early settlers quickly developed bottling, pickling and preserving skills, with cooks from different backgrounds swapping different ingredients and techniques – Malay sweetmeats, wonderful tropical Indian fruit chutneys and Dutch pickles and jams. Later imports expanded the influences – French distilling, German skills with yeast baking, and the British love of puddings. Baking is now enjoying a real resurgence. Artisan breads are being made in small bakeries with love, care and skilled hands, and Malay flatbreads and old-fashioned Dutch cake and chutney recipes are being revived in home kitchens.

# ARMMANS PUDDING

**Serves 6**

6 eggs

500g/1¼lb/2½ cups caster (superfine) sugar

500g/1¼lb/4½ cups plain (all-purpose) flour

10ml/2 tsp bicarbonate of soda (baking soda)

500ml/17fl oz/generous 2 cups full-fat (whole) milk, warm

125g/4¼oz/⅓ cup smooth apricot jam (see page 148)

125g/4¼oz/8½ tbsp butter, softened, plus extra for greasing

2.5ml/½ tsp lemon juice

**For the syrup**

2.5ml/½ tsp grated nutmeg

250g/9oz/1¼ cups caster (superfine) sugar

250ml/8fl oz/1 cup double (heavy) cream

250g/9oz/generous 1 cup butter

clotted cream or vanilla ice cream, to serve

This recipe is a more economical version of brandy pudding with the brandy omitted, which is how it gets its name – armmans is Dutch for 'poor man'. The dish shows the early settlers' love of 'konfyt', with apricot jam giving this dish a sticky texture and a sweet, warm tang.

**1** Preheat the oven to 180°C/350°F/Gas 4. Grease a deep, rectangular medium-sized baking dish with a little butter.

**2** Beat the eggs and sugar together in a large bowl until pale and creamy. Sift the flour and bicarbonate of soda together into the bowl, and gently fold into the mixture. Stir in the milk until the batter is thick and smooth.

**3** In a small bowl, mix the apricot jam, butter and lemon juice together, and gently fold this into the batter. Transfer to the baking dish. Bake in the oven for about 30–35 minutes until the pudding is risen and golden brown.

**4** While the pudding is baking prepare the syrup by mixing all the ingredients with 250ml/8fl oz/1 cup boiling water in a pan over a very gentle heat. Set aside to keep warm.

**5** Test whether the pudding is cooked by placing a skewer into the centre of the pudding, if it is ready it should come out clean. Remove from the oven and prick the pudding all over several times with a long skewer or a thin sharp knife. Pour the syrup over the cake; as it cools it will absorb the syrup.

**6** Spoon the warm pudding on to plates, and serve with a dollop of clotted cream or vanilla ice cream.

# MELKTERT

The milk for this tart is infused with vanilla and cinnamon, and adding a little sweet wine lifts the creaminess and adds a sophisticated note. We used Grand Constance wine from the much-vaunted Groot Constantia vineyard, part of the original farm that Simon Van der Stel established in 1685, and the oldest surviving wine farm in South Africa.

**Serves 8**

350g/12oz all-butter puff pastry

500ml/17fl oz/2 generous cups full-fat (whole) milk

1 stick of cinnamon, snapped

5ml/1 tsp vanilla bean paste or extract

4 eggs, lightly beaten

60ml/4 tbsp caster (superfine) sugar

25g/1oz/2 tbsp butter

15ml/1 tbsp cornflour (cornstarch), mixed with a little water

120ml/4fl oz/½ cup Grand Constance wine, or similar sauternes or muscat dessert wine

ground cinnamon and icing (confectioners') sugar, for dusting

**1** Roll out the puff pastry on a lightly-floured surface into a 35cm/14in circle. Line a 23cm/9in tart tin (pan) with the pastry, pushing it into the sides and bottom of the tin and leaving a little overhang to allow for shrinkage.

**2** Prick the base of the tin with a fork. Make an oversized circle of baking parchment and use it to line the tin. Add enough copper coins to cover the whole surface area of the base. Place in the freezer for 10 minutes to firm up the pastry. Place a baking sheet in the oven and preheat to 180°C/350°F/Gas 4.

**3** Place the chilled tart shell on the hot baking sheet in the oven and bake for 12–15 minutes, until the sides are a light golden colour. Remove the coins and parchment and return to the oven for a further 10 minutes until the base of the pastry is almost cooked. Remove from the oven and reduce the temperature to 150°C/300°F/Gas 2.

**4** In a medium pan, warm the milk with the cinnamon and vanilla bean paste. Beat the eggs and sugar in a mixing bowl until thick and creamy.

**5** Pour the warm, spiced milk over the eggs, mix well and return to the pan. Add the butter and the cornflour paste to the custard. Place on a medium heat and bring to a gentle simmer, stirring constantly. When the mixture starts to thicken, gradually stir in the wine.

**6** Remove the custard from the heat and allow to cool slightly before pouring into the baked tart shell. Slide the tart back into the oven and bake for 30–35 minutes; the tart should still be slightly wobbly. Dust with a little ground cinnamon and icing sugar and serve warm with cups of strong coffee.

*Cook's tip* The puff pastry is baked blind beforehand, so needs to be weighed down. Here we used coins instead of baking beans, as they are not only heavier they also conduct the heat better, which helps make the pastry base light and crisp.

*This 'milk tart' is an Old Cape Dutch speciality.*

# MALVA PUDDING WITH VAN DER HUM SAUCE

Of Cape Dutch origin this pudding is made with apricot jam and usually served with a similarly sweet and sticky sauce spiked with a little brandy liqueur such as South Africa's Van Der Hum liqueur. Admiral Van Der Hum was a noted member of the Dutch East India Company who was partial to a drop, or indeed barrel, of fortified brandy.

**Serves 6–8**

butter, for greasing

250g/9oz/1¼ cups caster (superfine) sugar

2 eggs

50g/2oz apricot jam (see page 148)

250g/9oz/2½ cups plain (all-purpose) flour

5ml/1 tsp bicarbonate of soda (baking soda)

250ml/8fl oz/1 cup full-fat (whole) milk

10ml/2 tsp white wine vinegar

5ml/1 tsp vanilla bean paste or extract

a pinch salt

**For the sauce**

250ml/8fl oz/1 cup double (heavy) cream

100g/3¾oz/½ cup white sugar

100g/3¾oz/scant ½ cup butter

50ml/2fl oz/¼ cup Van Der Hum liqueur (see page 154)

finely grated zest of 1 orange

**1** Preheat the oven to 180°C/350°F/Gas 4. Grease a 30 x 20cm/12 x 8in rectangular baking dish with butter.

**2** Beat the sugar and eggs together until pale, thick and creamy, then beat in the jam until well incorporated. Sift the flour and bicarbonate of soda together in a medium bowl, and add the salt. Mix the milk, vinegar and vanilla together in a separate bowl.

**3** Gradually fold the flour mixture into the beaten sugar and eggs, alternating with the milk mixture, until everything is well incorporated.

**4** Transfer the mixture into the prepared dish. Bake in the middle of the oven for 35–40 minutes. Test by inserting a skewer into the centre of the pudding, it should come out clean if it is ready. Keep the pudding warm.

**5** To make the sauce, combine all the ingredients in a pan over a low heat and stir continuously until all the sugar has dissolved. Boil rapidly for 2–3 minutes until the sauce thickens. Serve generous spoonfuls of the pudding with the sauce poured over.

*Sticky and sweet, malva pudding is a real winter warmer.*

# COCONUT TART

This is a tart with Dutch origins but refined by British settlers, who brought with them excellent pastry-making skills and recipes. It is a deliciously moist and moreish dessert, served here with peaches cooked on the braai. Traditionally the filling is made with water but here we enhanced the sweet coconut flavour with coconut milk. Serve with an ostentatious dollop of thick cream, coconut ice cream or sorbet.

**Serves 6–8**

**For the tart**
250g/9oz ready-rolled all-butter puff pastry
1 egg, lightly beaten
115g/4oz/½ cup butter
200g/7oz/1 cup white sugar
2 eggs, lightly beaten
250g/9oz/1 cup desiccated (dry unsweetened shredded) coconut
225ml/7½fl oz/1 cup coconut milk
75ml/5 tbsp apricot jam

**For the peaches**
6 ripe peaches, halved and stone (pit) removed
45ml/3 tbsp butter, melted
15ml/1 tbsp vanilla bean paste or extract
thick double (heavy) cream or ice cream, to serve

**1** Preheat an oven to 200°C/400°F/Gas 6. Line a flat baking sheet with baking parchment. Place the pastry on the lined baking sheet.

**2** With a small knife, score a border 2cm/¾in from the edge of the pastry. With a fork prick inside the border of the pastry all over. Brush a little beaten egg around the border of the pastry. Place in the refrigerator for 10 minutes to chill, then bake blind in the oven for 12–15 minutes until the border of the pastry is lightly golden and well risen. Gently push the centre down a little so it settles into the border of the tart shell, then set aside to cool.

**3** To make the filling, cream the butter and sugar together until light and creamy. Add the eggs gradually, whisking well between additions. Add the desiccated coconut and coconut milk. Mix until well combined.

**4** Turn the oven down to 160°C/325°F/Gas 3. Spread a generous layer of jam over the base, then spoon the coconut mixture on top, spreading evenly across the surface. Place in the oven for 25–30 minutes until the filling has set and is slightly golden on top but moist in the centre.

**5** Meanwhile prepare the peaches; mix the butter and vanilla in a small bowl and brush the peaches all over with a little butter. Place on a buttered sheet of foil and seal the parcel up, then place on a medium hot braai, but not directly over the coals, for about 20 minutes. They can also be baked in the oven at the same time as you are baking the tart. Remove the peaches from their skins when cooked, if you wish.

**6** Cut the tart into generous slices, and serve warm with the peaches and a spoonful of cream or ice cream.

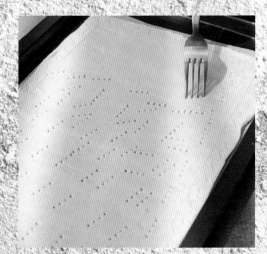

This recipe uses yellow-fleshed cling peaches, which are ideal for cooking as they have a sweet but firm flesh.

# KOEKSISTERS

**Makes 12**

250g/9oz/1¼ cups plain (all-purpose) flour
15ml/1 tbsp baking powder
2.5ml/½ tsp salt
5ml/1 tsp ground cinnamon
2.5ml/½ tsp ground ginger
30ml/2 tbsp butter, cut into small cubes
2 eggs
125ml/4fl oz/½ cup buttermilk
corn oil, for deep frying

**For the syrup**

250g/9oz/1¼ cups white sugar
15ml/1 tbsp rosewater
30ml/2 tbsp dried naartjie or mandarin peel
3 cardamom pods, bruised
5cm/1in piece fresh root ginger, sliced
1 cinnamon stick, snapped in half
zest of 1 lemon

The recipe for these lovely little pastries, similar to a doughnut in texture, combines a classic colonial recipe with Malay aromatics. The spiced syrup should be made a day in advance so that the flavours have time to develop.

**1** To make the syrup, place all the ingredients together with 250ml/8fl oz/1 cup water into a heavy pan. Stir over a low heat until the sugar has been dissolved. Boil rapidly for 3–4 minutes and set aside to cool, preferably overnight.

**2** To make the dough, sift the flour, baking powder, salt and spices into a large mixing bowl and using the tips of your fingers, rub in the butter until the mixture resembles fine breadcrumbs.

**3** Whisk the eggs and buttermilk together and slowly incorporate them into the flour mixture. Tip the dough on to a lightly floured surface and knead gently until the mixture is stretchy and silky. Set aside in a bowl, cover with clear film (plastic wrap) and leave in a warm place for an hour or so.

**4** Tip the dough out and knock back (punch down) for a minute until the dough is smooth and elastic. Roll the dough into a large rectangle 40 x 25cm/16 x 10in. Cut into smaller rectangles of about 10 x 3cm/5 x 1½in. Leaving 1cm/½in at the top intact, cut each little rectangle into 3 strips. Plait (braid) the 3 strips over each other in turn, pressing together firmly at the end.

**5** Heat the oil in a pan or deep-fat fryer to 180°C/350°F. In batches, so you don't crowd them, carefully lower the koeksisters into the hot oil and cook for 3–4 minutes until golden all over. Remove with a slotted spoon and drain well on kitchen paper.

**6** Place the still warm koeksisters into the cool syrup and turn until they are well coated and have slightly absorbed the syrup, then remove and place on a cooling rack to drain and cool. Serve with hot coffee or refreshing rooibos tea.

*Koeksisters is Old Dutch for cookies ...*

# AMARULA NUT TRUFFLES

This recipe is an ode to the fusion cooking traditions of South Africa, as it contains Amarula, macadamias, Kalahari salt and Cape Town chocolate. Macadamia nuts are native to New South Wales, Australia, but have been farmed with great success in South Africa, while Amarula cream liqueur is made from the fruit of the marula tree, unique to sub-Saharan Africa, and Kalahari salt is taken from an undisturbed ancient saltpan under the desert. Cape Town has many great artisan chocolate producers and chocolatiers, including Honest Chocolate, which uses raw cocoa and agave nectar rather than sugar in all their confections. Serve these rich truffles with thick espresso coffee.

**Makes about 24**

450g/1lb good quality 70 per cent
dark (bittersweet) chocolate,
roughly chopped

250ml/8fl oz/1 cup double
(heavy) cream

75g/3oz/6 tbsp butter

5ml/1 tsp Kalahari salt or other good-
quality salt flakes, such as Malden

50ml/2fl oz/¼ cup Amarula liqueur

150g/5oz/1¼ cups macadamia nuts,
toasted and finely chopped

**1** Chop 250g/9oz of the chocolate and place in a large heatproof bowl. Heat the cream, butter and salt in a pan over a low heat until the cream just comes to the boil, then quickly pour the hot cream over the chocolate.

**2** Stir the cream and chocolate, mixing in a tight circle until the chocolate starts to melt and emulsify with the cream. Mix in the Amarula; you should now have a thick and shiny ganache. Place the ganache in the refrigerator, mixing every 20 minutes until the mixture is just set.

**3** Form the ganache into truffle shapes using either a melon spoon or a teaspoon and set aside on a tray lined with baking parchment. Chill in the refrigerator to firm up a little.

**4** Melt the remaining chocolate in a heatproof bowl set over a pan of simmering water, without stirring, or in the microwave, and set aside to cool.

**5** Place the toasted macadamia nuts on a plate or in a shallow bowl. Dip the chilled truffles into the melted chocolate, remove with a fork and drain them a little, then roll in the macadamia nuts. Place the truffles on baking parchment and chill again to firm up a little. They can then be kept in a cool, dry dark place for up to 1 week.

# BUTTERNUT SQUASH BREAD

South Africa's butternut squash is grown all over the country and its season is a year-round phenomenon. Using a little mealie meal on the baking sheet will give a lovely crispy base. Take a loaf on a picnic with cold meats, pickles, atjar and fresh salads, or serve as an appetizer with a sage and chilli dipping oil, as here.

**Makes 2 x 800g/1¾lb loaves**

500g/1¼lb butternut squash,
peeled, seeded and diced

400ml/14fl oz/1⅔ cups
full-fat (whole) milk

2.5ml/½ tsp ground cinnamon

1.5ml/¼ tsp grated nutmeg

5ml/1 tsp cumin seeds,
lightly crushed

salt and pepper

800g/1¾lb/7 cups strong white
bread flour

15g/½oz/1 tbsp active dried yeast

10ml/2 tsp fine salt

mealie meal, or semolina,
for sprinkling

1 egg, beaten

**For the sage and chilli
dipping oil**

60ml/4 tbsp virgin olive oil

about 12 medium sage leaves

1 small red chilli, deseeded
and finely chopped

**1** In a medium pan place the diced squash and milk, add the cinnamon, nutmeg and cumin and cook over a gentle heat for about 20 minutes until the squash is tender. Blend the squash and milk together using a hand blender or food processor, season with salt and pepper and set aside to cool a little.

**2** In a large bowl, sift the flour, yeast and salt. Make a well in the middle and add the milk and mashed squash mixture, folding in until incorporated.

**3** Tip out on to a floured surface and knead for about 10–15 minutes until the mixture is smooth and elastic, adding a little more flour if the dough is too soft and sticky. This can also be done in a mixing bowl with a dough hook.

**4** Place the dough into a lightly greased bowl, cover with a clean dish towel and place in a warm place until the mixture has almost doubled in size.

**5** Knock back (punch down) the dough with your fist to remove any excess air. Tip out on to a lightly floured board or surface and knead until it is smooth and elastic. Cut the dough into equal halves and form into 2 oval loaf shapes.

**6** Place the loaves on a baking sheet sprinkled with a little mealie meal. Brush the tops with a little beaten egg and make diagonal slashes in the loaves with a serrated knife. Cover loosely with clear film (plastic wrap) and set aside in a warm place for about 30–35 minutes to prove.

**7** Preheat the oven to 190°C/400°F/Gas 5. When the loaves have roughly doubled in size, bake in the oven for 30–35 minutes until well risen and golden and the bottom of the loaves sound hollow when tapped. Cool on a wire rack for at least 20 minutes.

**8** Meanwhile make the chilli oil: warm the oil in a small frying pan over a medium heat. When the oil is hot, drop in the sage leaves and chilli; as soon as they sizzle, remove from the heat. Leave to infuse and cool then transfer to a serving bowl. Serve the bread in slices or hunks, dipped into the chilli oil.

*This recipe is a great way to use up leftover roasted squash ...*

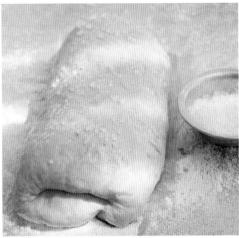

# BEER BREAD

### Makes 1 x 800g/1¾lb loaf

200g/7oz potatoes, peeled and grated

30ml/2 tbsp demerara (raw) sugar

10ml/2 tsp active dried yeast

350g/12oz/3 cups strong white bread flour

5ml/1 tsp salt

10ml/2 tsp white sugar

30ml/2 tbsp olive oil, plus a little extra for greasing

250ml/8fl oz/1 cup wheat beer

1 egg, lightly beaten, for brushing

fig konfyt (see page 142) and a soft cheese such as camembert, for serving

Traditionally, European South African settlers made a yeast culture with potatoes for baking, and this recipe uses a starter with grated potatoes to help develop a similar authentic flavour. We also used Wild Beast ale, a superb wheat beer and one of the great quality craft brews of South Africa.

**1** First make the starter. Put the potatoes with 300ml/½ pint/1¼ cups of water into a small pan. Bring to the boil, remove from the heat, and pour into an airtight container with a tight-fitting lid. Allow it to cool to blood temperature before adding the demerara sugar and 5ml/1 tsp yeast, cover and leave in a warm place overnight. Use as required, it will keep for up to 1 week.

**2** Sift the flour and salt into a large mixing bowl, stir in the white sugar and 5ml/1 tsp yeast, then add 90ml/6 tbsp of starter with the oil and wheat beer. Mix to form a smooth, stiff dough. You could use the dough hook attachment on a food processor.

**3** Turn out on to a lightly floured surface and work the dough for about 10 minutes to develop the gluten and to make the dough smooth, stretchy and elastic. Grease the bowl with a little oil, place the dough into the bowl and cover with a damp dish towel. Leave in a warm place to prove for about 1 hour until the dough has doubled in size.

**4** Preheat the oven to 180°C/350°F/Gas 4. Knock back (punch down) the dough and knead for 2–3 minutes until the dough is soft and silken to touch. Form into a lozenge shape and place on a lightly oiled baking sheet.

**5** Brush the top of the loaf with beaten egg and make diagonal slashes with a serrated knife on the top. Loosely cover with clear film (plastic wrap) and leave in a warm place for about 20–30 minutes to prove.

**6** When the loaf has risen, transfer to the oven and bake for 30–35 minutes until golden, well risen and it sounds hollow when knocked on the base. Cool on a wire rack for 20 minutes. Slice and serve with soft cheese and fig konfyt.

*The dough for this bread is enriched with buttermilk and eggs ...*

# PICNIC BREAD
# AND MASON JAR SALAD

This bread has a dense and rich texture that is almost a meal in itself, which makes it ideal to take on the road or indeed to the beach, together with an equally portable jar of salad. You can experiment with different flavourings in the loaf, like roasted vegetables or goat's cheese. This version is accompanied by a mason jar salad of tomato, roasted butternut squash, pumpkin seeds and feta, a nutritious lunch for travelling voortrekkers.

**Serves 4**

525g/1lb 5oz/5 cups strong white bread flour
2.5ml/½ tsp fine salt
5ml/1 tsp white sugar
7.5ml/1½ tsp active dried yeast
3 eggs, beaten
200ml/7fl oz/scant 1 cup warm water
75ml/2½fl oz/⅓ cup buttermilk
4 spring onions (scallions), trimmed and finely chopped
150g/5oz Cheddar cheese, grated
175g/6oz smoked streaky (fatty) bacon, cooked and finely chopped
30ml/2 tbsp chopped fresh sage
15ml/1 tbsp chopped fresh rosemary
15ml/1 tbsp fresh thyme leaves
sunflower oil, for greasing

**For the mason jar salad**
300g/11oz butternut squash, cut into 2cm/1in cubes
60ml/4 tbsp pumpkin oil
110g/4oz vine-ripened cherry tomatoes
30ml/2 tbsp pumpkin seeds, lightly toasted
50g/2oz feta cheese, crumbled
50ml/2fl oz/¼ cup olive oil
15ml/1 tbsp lemon juice
2 cloves garlic, crushed
50g/2oz rocket (arugula) leaves
salt and black pepper

**1** To make the bread, mix the flour, salt, sugar and yeast into a large mixing bowl and make a well in the centre of the flour. In a separate bowl combine the eggs, water and buttermilk. Pour the buttermilk mixture gradually into the well in the flour, and mix until a soft dough is formed.

**2** Transfer the dough on to a lightly floured surface and knead for 5 minutes until smooth and elastic. Place in a lightly oiled bowl, cover with clear film (plastic wrap) and leave in a warm place for 35 minutes until doubled in size.

**3** In a bowl, mix together the spring onions, grated cheese, bacon and herbs. When the dough is ready, knock back (punch down) a little in the bowl then tip out and knead until silky and smooth. Pull and stretch the dough to a flat disk. Sprinkle over the bacon and cheese mixture, fold into the dough, then knead until evenly distributed.

**4** Shape the dough into a long oval and place on to an oiled baking sheet or place in a lightly oiled 1kg/2lb loaf tin (pan). Cover loosely with clear film and leave in a warm place for 30 minutes to allow the dough to grow and prove.

**5** Preheat the oven to 200°C/400°F/Gas 6. Place the loaf into the oven and bake for 25–30 minutes until well risen and golden. Tap the base to ensure the bread is cooked, it should sound hollow. Cool for at least 30 minutes.

**6** To make the salad, roast the butternut squash in pumpkin oil in a roasting pan for 25 minutes, until tender and golden. Add the tomatoes and return to the oven for a further 10 minutes, adding the pumpkin seeds for the last 5 minutes; the squash should now be slightly charred around the edges. Allow to cool, then decant into a large clean jar with a wide top. Add the feta cheese in a layer on top.

**7** Make the dressing in a small bowl by whisking together the olive oil, lemon juice and garlic, seasoning with a little salt and pepper. Pour the dressing over the cheese, add the rocket leaves on top, and seal with the lid. Gently mix before serving with slices of picnic bread.

# WESTERN CAPE GREEN FIG KONFYT

Figs were brought to South Africa by the Dutch, who planted the fruit trees at stages along the Western Cape so that east-bound sailors could restock their ships. The fruits are a remarkable source of calcium, which might explain why the Dutch were so keen to grow and then preserve them. Serve the konfyt with soft cheese, as a dessert with whipped cream, or as a breakfast treat with thick yogurt and almonds.

*Figs are the most mentioned fruit in the bible ...*

**Makes 1kg/2¼lb**

500g/1¼lb green figs
30ml/2 tbsp sea salt
15ml/1 tbsp bicarbonate of soda
(baking soda)
500g/1¼lb/3 cups white sugar
2 cinnamon sticks
1 vanilla pod (bean), split lengthways

**1** Trim the top of the figs of any excess stem. Cut a deep crisscross in the base of each fig and place in a large bowl. Cover with cold water and add the salt. Leave to soak overnight.

**2** The next day remove the figs from the water. Bring a large pan of fresh water and the bicarbonate of soda to the boil. Add the figs and simmer very gently, so the figs aren't moving, for 20–30 minutes until just tender. Remove and cool quickly in iced water. Drain and place in a large preserving pan.

**3** Make the syrup by placing the sugar, 75ml/5 tbsp water, the cinnamon and vanilla pod in a heavy pan. Stir over a low heat until the sugar has dissolved, increase the heat and boil for 5 minutes, then pour over the figs. Cover the pan, reduce the heat, and simmer gently for 1 hour until the figs are soft.

**4** Meanwhile prepare your jars by washing them well and then sterilizing them in the oven at 110°C/225°F/Gas ¼ for 20 minutes.

**5** Lift the figs out of the pan with a slotted spoon and place them in the warm jars. Continue to cook the syrup for 5 minutes more then pour over the figs and seal. Enjoy with whipped cream as a dessert, or make a crunchy granola and serve with thick Greek (US strained plain) yogurt for a breakfast treat.

*Cook's tip* Fully ripened figs are too delicate to survive the cooking process, so the figs for this recipe must be picked or bought when they are still hard and green.

The quince is thought to have been introduced to South Africa by Jan Van Riebeeck and the trees were planted with great success in gardens throughout Cape Town.

# QUINCE JAM

This jam, which unlike a quince jelly should have a grainy texture, makes an excellent accompaniment to roast meats and cheeses, or spread on fish for a braai. When quinces are in season they also make a wonderful quickly prepared dessert: halved, sprinkled with brown sugar and microwaved for a few minutes.

**Makes 1 litre/1¾ pints/4 cups**

1kg/2¼lb quinces, washed, stalks removed, and sliced into eighths

about 800g/1¾lb/3¾ cups white sugar

45ml/3 tbsp preserved stem ginger, thinly sliced

4 allspice berries, lightly crushed

3 cloves

1 star anise

rind from 1 lemon, peeled into strips

**1** Clean and sterilize your jars in the dishwasher or wash them thoroughly in hot soapy water, rinse and place them in an oven at 110°C/225°F/Gas ¼ for 15 minutes. Keep warm and set aside.

**2** Place the quinces in a large pan of cold water and slowly bring to the boil. Simmer for about 45–50 minutes until the quinces are soft and pulpy. Remove from the water and push through a sieve (strainer) into a clean bowl, making sure all the pulp goes through.

**3** Measure the quantity of quince purée by volume, and calculate and measure out 400ml/14fl oz/1⅔ cups of sugar for every 500ml/17fl oz/generous 2 cups of purée. Place in a heavy pan or preserving pan. Wrap the spices and lemon strips in a piece of muslin (cheesecloth), tie securely and add to the preserving pan. Cook over a low heat, stirring until the sugar is dissolved.

**4** Bring the jam to a rapid boil. Cook for about 10 minutes, stirring every so often, until it reaches 110°C/225°F with a sugar thermometer.

**5** Ladle the jam into the clean warm jars and seal. Place the sealed jars in a pan and simmer for 15 minutes to seal the jars tightly. Keep in a cool, dry dark cupboard for up to 1 year.

# APRICOT JAM

Appearing in many recipes, as well as eaten all year round on bread and toast, apricot jam is ubiquitous in South African cuisine. It is not only a key ingredient, it also crosses the boundaries of savoury to sweet, and of condiment to konfyt. In this version, adding a few apricot kernels to the jam gives an almond-like nuttiness to the end result.

**Makes 1.75 litres/
3 pints/7½ cups**

1.8kg/4lb apricots, washed
juice of 1 lemon
1.8kg/4lb/8 cups golden
caster (superfine) sugar
a small knob of butter

**1** Clean and sterilize your jars in the dishwasher or wash them thoroughly in hot soapy water, rinse and place them in an oven at 110°C/225°F/Gas ¼ for 15 minutes. Keep warm and set aside.

**2** Cut the apricots in half and remove the stones (pits). Keep 10 of the stones and discard the rest. Place the halved apricots and lemon juice into a large preserving pan.

**3** To remove the apricot kernel from the stone, place on a chopping board and hit with a hammer to split the outer shell, prise out the kernel and discard the shells. Blanch the kernels in boiling water for 1 minute. Drain, refresh and chop finely. Add to the apricots in the pan.

**4** Pour about 900ml/1½ pints/3¾ cups of water into the pan, and add the sugar. Bring to a simmer and cook for 15–20 minutes until the sugar is completely dissolved and the apricots are broken down and pulpy. Stir in the butter, then skim the surface of the jam to remove any scum.

**5** Test for the setting point by dropping a teaspoon of the jam on to a cold plate and push with your finger; if it wrinkles it is ready. Then ladle the jam into the warm jars. Seal and store in a cool, dark place for up to 2 years.

# PINEAPPLE AND GINGER BEER WITH PUMPKIN PIPS

This beer is best made overnight and consumed within 2 days, and can be served poured over crushed ice. Sweet pineapple flesh gives a great contrast to warm spices like ginger and chillies, and in some parts of the Eastern Cape it is sprinkled with chilli powder and eaten as a refreshing snack when the sun is hot. Adding a little cayenne pepper and salt to the pumpkin pips gives a little warmth that helps the pineapple beer slip down beautifully.

**Makes about 4 litres/
8½ pints/16 cups**

**For the beer**
2 medium-ripe pineapples,
peeled and chopped
1.5kg/3¼lb/7 cups caster
(superfine) sugar
75ml/5 tbsp ground ginger
50g/2oz sultanas (golden raisins)
15ml/1 tbsp bicarbonate of soda
(baking soda)
10ml/2 tsp active dried yeast
sliced pineapple and pineapple
leaves, to garnish

**For the pumpkin pips**
200g/7oz pumpkin seeds
5ml/1 tsp coarse flaked sea salt
10ml/2 tsp cayenne pepper,
or to taste
finely grated zest of 1 lemon

**1** To make the pineapple beer, place the pineapple in a large bowl or container. Add 5 litres/9 pints tepid water, the sugar, ginger, sultanas and bicarbonate of soda and mix well. Add the yeast, cover with a clean damp towel and leave in a dark cool place for 24 hours; the raisins should start floating to the top.

**2** Prepare your bottles and lids by washing thoroughly, and sterilizing in an oven at 110°C/225°F/Gas ¼ or alternatively by using the highest heat setting on your dishwasher.

**3** Strain the fermented beer through a fine sieve (strainer) and decant into clean bottles. Chill very well before serving.

**4** To make the pumpkin pips, preheat the oven to 180°C/350°F/Gas 4. Place the pumpkin seeds on a baking sheet and roast in the oven for about 5 minutes until the skin changes colour from a deep dark green to brown.

**5** Remove and sprinkle with salt, cayenne pepper and lemon zest. Place in a clean airtight container until ready to serve with your drinks. They will keep for about 2 weeks.

**6** Serve the beer with a little crushed ice in a frosted glass, garnished with slices of pineapple and some pineapple leaves and accompanied by a little dish of pumpkin pips.

ROOIBOS ICE
TEA COCKTAIL

Rooibos has a mellow, slightly sweet and nut-like flavour that South Africans have been drinking and cooking with since the 18th century, and the tea is enjoyed by everyone from Durban to Noordhoek. This rooibos cocktail can be shaken and served over ice or straight up, martini-style.

**Serves 2**

45ml/3 tbsp rooibos tea leaves

45ml/3 tbsp caster (superfine) sugar

2.5ml/½ tsp finely grated lime zest

2.5ml/½ tsp finely grated orange zest

1 egg white

25ml/1½ tbsp South African brandy

25ml/1½ tbsp dark rum

25ml/1½ tbsp orange liqueur such as Grand Mariner

25ml/1½ tbsp freshly squeezed orange juice

25ml/1½ tbsp freshly squeezed lime juice

ice cubes, cinnamon or regular cola and sprigs of mint, to serve

**1** Prepare the tea ahead so it can be chilled for a few hours. Bring your kettle to a rolling boil and pour 300ml/½ pint/1¼ cups water on to the leaves. Leave to infuse for 3–5 minutes, then strain into a measuring jug (cup). Cool and store in the refrigerator until ready to use.

**2** When ready to make the cocktail, first prepare the glasses. Mix the sugar and grated zests together on a large dinner plate. Place the egg white in a bowl.

**3** Invert the rim of the glasses into the egg white and move around for a couple of seconds so that the rim has an even coating of egg white. Lift the glass and move it to the plate of sugar and zest mixture, pressing down to coat and allow the sugar to absorb. Leave the glasses inverted until the sugar has dried.

**4** To mix the cocktails measure the brandy, rum and orange liqueur into a 1.5 litre/2½ pint/6¼ cup jug or pitcher. Add the chilled tea, orange juice and lime juice. Top up with ice cubes and stir. Add cola to taste.

**5** Pour the cocktail into the prepared glasses and top up with a little more cola if desired. Garnish with sprigs of fresh mint.

*Rooibos tea, grown exclusively in the Cederberg region of the Western Cape, makes a refreshing and distinctive drink cold as well as hot.*

# VAN DER HUM-STYLE LIQUEUR

Made from South African brandy, Van Der Hum liqueur was named after the Dutch admiral who was so fond of this blend of brandy, citrus and spices that his crewmen named the drink after him. It is a wonderfully sweet and spicy drink, which can be enjoyed simply with ice, served as a frappé with orange sorbet, or made into a Van Der Hum coffee.

**Makes 800ml/1½ pints/3¼ cups**

150g/5oz/¾ cup golden caster (superfine) sugar
1 cinnamon stick
5 whole cloves
1.5ml/¼ tsp freshly grated nutmeg
3 cardamom pods, lightly bruised
750ml/1¼ pints/3 cups brandy
25g/1oz dried naartjie or mandarin peel
50ml/2fl oz/¼ cup dark spiced rum
5 orange blossoms (if available), or a few drops of orange blossom water

**1** Clean and sterilize a large bottle thoroughly by washing in hot soapy water, rinsing and then placing in an oven at 110°C/225°F/Gas ¼ for 15 minutes, or washing in a dishwasher at the highest temperature setting. Ensure you have a clean well-fitting lid with a new seal.

**2** Place the sugar in a small pan and add 45ml/3 tbsp cold water. Over a low heat, stir until the sugar has dissolved. Remove from the heat and pour into the sterilized bottle.

**3** Snap the cinnamon stick and place it and the rest of the spices into the bottle. Add the brandy, naartjie peel, rum and orange blossoms or orange blossom water.

**4** Store in a cool dark place, shaking gently every few days for 1 month, then decant into a clean, sterilized bottle and seal. Serve with ice for an aperitif, accompanied by some sliced cured meats and a few olives.

South Africa produces about half the amount of brandy that the Cognac region in France does, however little or none of it is for export. Historically, South African brandy had a poor and primitive image, but in the late 19th century, with the arrival of a Frenchman named René Santhagens who trained in Cognac, the transformation of South African brandy distilling began. He revolutionized the industry, resulting in a more consistent, complex and flavoursome spirit that Van Der Hum himself would have approved of.

# NUTRITIONAL NOTES

The nutritional analysis given for each recipe is calculated per portion (i.e. serving or item), unless otherwise stated. If the recipe gives a range, such as serves 4–6, the nutritional analysis will be for the smaller portion size, i.e. 6 servings. The analysis does not include optional ingredients, such as salt added to taste.

**Braai-baked pot bread:** (makes 1kg/2¼lb loaf) Energy 2046kcal/ 8666kJ; Protein 58.1g; Carbohydrate 399g, of which sugars 17.6g; Fat 35.3g, of which saturates 6g; Cholesterol 231mg; Calcium 748mg; Fibre 20.7g; Sodium 2072mg.

**Snoek, mealies and potatoes on the braai:** (serves 4) Energy 1444kcal/6020kJ; Protein 78.4g; Carbohydrate 74.6g, of which sugars 33.9g; Fat 94.3g, of which saturates 33g; Cholesterol 281mg; Calcium 109mg; Fibre 8.1g; Sodium 585mg.

**Grilled yellowtail in banana leaf:** (serves 4) Energy 323kcal/1347kJ; Protein 38.5g; Carbohydrate 3.1g, of which sugars 2.5g; Fat 17.4g, of which saturates 10g; Cholesterol 92mg; Calcium 34mg; Fibre 0.6g; Sodium 125mg.

**Beer can peri-peri chicken:** (serves 4–5) Energy 651kcal/2698kJ; Protein 50.2g; Carbohydrate 1.1g, of which sugars 1g; Fat 49.4g, of which saturates 11.9g; Cholesterol 264mg; Calcium 37mg; Fibre 0.6g; Sodium 578mg.

**The burger:** (serves 6) Energy 567kcal/2369kJ; Protein 45.3g; Carbohydrate 22.3g, of which sugars 1.5g; Fat 33.8g, of which saturates 15.7g; Cholesterol 134mg; Calcium 341mg; Fibre 2.7g; Sodium 593mg.

**Prego roll:** (serves 2) Energy 557kcal/2328kJ; Protein 38g; Carbohydrate 27.7g, of which sugars 4.3g; Fat 32.4g, of which saturates 6.4g; Cholesterol 89mg; Calcium 70mg; Fibre 2g; Sodium 360mg.

**Boerewors with tomato sauce:** (serves 8) Energy 623kcal/2588kJ; Protein 22.9g; Carbohydrate 22g, of which sugars 9.2g; Fat 49.9g, of which saturates 17.6g; Cholesterol 113mg; Calcium 206mg; Fibre 1.1g; Sodium 1620mg.

**Steak with monkey gland sauce:** (serves 4–6) Energy 515kcal/2146kJ; Protein 37.8g; Carbohydrate 20.8g, of which sugars 18.6g; Fat 29.9g, of which saturates 8.6g; Cholesterol 99mg; Calcium 53mg; Fibre 3.1g; Sodium 376mg.

**Karoo lamb with lavender:** (serves 8) Energy 520kcal/2183kJ; Protein 78.3g; Carbohydrate 0g, of which sugars 0g; Fat 23g, of which saturates 9.3g; Cholesterol 275mg; Calcium 20mg; Fibre 0g; Sodium 155mg.

**Lamb sosaties:** (serves 4) Energy 616kcal/2585kJ; Protein 53.6g; Carbohydrate 44.7g, of which sugars 44.7g; Fat 26g, of which saturates 9.4g; Cholesterol 185mg; Calcium 87mg; Fibre 6.3g; Sodium 197mg.

**Karoo ostrich potjie:** (serves 6–8) Energy 441kcal/1854kJ; Protein 61.5g; Carbohydrate 13.6g, of which sugars 7.2g; Fat 13.9g, of which saturates 4.4g; Cholesterol 139mg; Calcium 59mg; Fibre 3.4g; Sodium 628mg

**Snoek sambal:** (serves 4) Energy 474kcal/1969kJ; Protein 13.9g; Carbohydrate 23g, of which sugars 7.8g; Fat 36.9g, of which saturates 16.3g; Cholesterol 106mg; Calcium 90mg; Fibre 3.3g; Sodium 689mg.

**Plettenberg bay squid:** (serves 4) Energy 261kcal/1096kJ; Protein 23.4g; Carbohydrate 16.7g, of which sugars 13.3g; Fat 11.6g, of which saturates 1.7g; Cholesterol 281mg; Calcium 146mg; Fibre 5.9g; Sodium 269mg.

**Peri-peri crayfish:** (serves 4–6) Energy 259kcal/1072kJ; Protein 8.8g; Carbohydrate 7.1g, of which sugars 6.2g; Fat 21.9g, of which saturates 5.8g; Cholesterol 53mg; Calcium 43mg; Fibre 2.6g; Sodium 162mg.

**Snoek kedgeree:** (serves 4) Energy 762kcal/3176kJ; Protein 33.1g; Carbohydrate 61.7g, of which sugars 18.6g; Fat 43g, of which saturates 22.5g; Cholesterol 275mg; Calcium 133mg; Fibre 6.3g; Sodium 869mg.

**Fish bobotie:** (serves 4) Energy 311kcal/1305kJ; Protein 25.7g; Carbohydrate 20.7g, of which sugars 12.9g; Fat 14.5g, of which saturates 4g; Cholesterol 183mg; Calcium 177mg; Fibre 1.5g; Sodium 281mg.

**Tea-smoked Drakensberg trout:** (serves 4) Energy 357kcal/1486kJ; Protein 34.6g; Carbohydrate 3.5g, of which sugars 1.3g; Fat 24.7g, of which saturates 3.1g; Cholesterol 44mg; Calcium 119mg; Fibre 0g; Sodium 2357mg.

**Lamb bobotie:** (serves 6) Energy 585kcal/2441kJ; Protein 40g; Carbohydrate 25.9g, of which sugars 19g; Fat 36.4g, of which saturates 14.2g; Cholesterol 289mg; Calcium 97mg; Fibre 1g; Sodium 264mg.

**Tomato bredie with amasi raita:** (serves 6–8) Energy 380kcal/1591kJ; Protein 29.4g; Carbohydrate 24.4g, of which sugars 13g; Fat 19g, of which saturates 9.3g; Cholesterol 126mg; Calcium 100mg; Fibre 4.3g; Sodium 350mg.

**Samoosas:** (serves 8) Energy 246kcal/ 1029kJ; Protein 9.7g; Carbohydrate 24.8g, of which sugars 5.5g; Fat 12.8g, of which saturates 2.8g; Cholesterol 19mg; Calcium 94mg; Fibre 3g; Sodium 34mg.

**Bunny chow with coriander chutney:** (serves 4) Energy 956kcal/4038kJ; Protein 47.2g; Carbohydrate 131.6g, of which sugars 16.5g; Fat 30.8g, of which saturates 9g; Cholesterol 132mg; Calcium 313mg; Fibre 8.7g; Sodium 1185mg.

**Chicken and prawn curry:** (serves 4) Energy 500kcal/2096kJ; Protein 34.3g; Carbohydrate 58.5g, of which sugars 13.5g; Fat 14.5g, of which saturates 2.4g; Cholesterol 110mg; Calcium 142mg; Fibre 5.5g; Sodium 261mg.

**Kudu pie:** (serves 4) Energy 965kcal/4031kJ; Protein 47.2g; Carbohydrate 63.4g, of which sugars 21.4g; Fat 57.6g, of which saturates 32.2g; Cholesterol 215mg; Calcium 125mg; Fibre 3.7g; Sodium 778mg.

**Game and beef biltong:** (makes 1kg/ 2lb) Energy 2074kcal/8801kJ; Protein 444.3g; Carbohydrate 3.4g, of which sugars 3.2g; Fat 32g, of which saturates 16g; Cholesterol 1000mg; Calcium 142mg; Fibre 0g; Sodium 1364mg.

**Springbok carpaccio:** (serves 4) Energy 178kcal/736kJ; Protein 11.3g; Carbohydrate 0.2g, of which sugars 0.2g; Fat 14.6g, of which saturates 2.4g; Cholesterol 25mg; Calcium 15mg; Fibre 0.4g; Sodium 30mg.

**Roasted butternut squash soup:** (serves 6) Energy 92kcal/388kJ; Protein 2.9g; Carbohydrate 19.4g, of which sugars 12.8g; Fat 1g, of which saturates 0.1g; Cholesterol 0mg; Calcium 73mg; Fibre 4.5g; Sodium 288mg.

**Mealie croquettes:** (serves 8) Energy 524kcal/2197kJ; Protein 14.7g; Carbohydrate 79.9g, of which sugars 33.3g; Fat 16.7g, of which saturates 3.6g; Cholesterol 26mg; Calcium 81mg; Fibre 7.5g; Sodium 156mg.

**Mealie curry with parathas:** (serves 4) Energy 1071kcal/4471kJ; Protein 16.8g; Carbohydrate 107.4g, of which sugars 14.6g; Fat 67g, of which saturates 34.5g; Cholesterol 133mg; Calcium 225mg; Fibre 8.7g; Sodium 506mg.

**Setjesta:** (serves 4) Energy 527kcal/2201kJ; Protein 11.2g; Carbohydrate 60g, of which sugars 19.5g; Fat 27.5g, of which saturates 13.5g; Cholesterol 57mg; Calcium 272mg; Fibre 7.3g; Sodium 194mg.

**Blatjang:** (makes 3kg/6½lb) Energy 4650kcal/19890kJ; Protein 18g; Carbohydrate 1191g, of which sugars 1122g; Fat 0g, of which saturates 0g; Cholesterol 0mg; Calcium 750mg; Fibre 0g; Sodium 24000mg.

**Pickled achard:** (serves 4–6) Energy 270kcal/1118kJ; Protein 6g; Carbohydrate 15g, of which sugars 11g; Fat 21g, of which saturates 4.1g; Cholesterol 0mg; Calcium 93mg; Fibre 5.8g; Sodium 32mg.

**Heritage tomato chutney:** (makes 1.75 litres/3 pints/7½ cups) Energy 2988kcal/12672kJ; Protein 19.8g; Carbohydrate 734.4g, of which sugars 723.6g; Fat 5.4g, of which saturates 1.1g; Cholesterol 0mg; Calcium 396mg; Fibre 31.2g; Sodium 2340mg.

**Mango and peach atjar:** (makes 500ml/17fl oz/2 cups) Energy 945kcal/4030kJ; Protein 3.5g; Carbohydrate 241.5g, of which sugars 228.5g; Fat 0.5g, of which saturates 0g; Cholesterol 0mg; Calcium 45mg; Fibre 0g; Sodium 6500mg.

**Banana sambal:** (serves 4) Energy 94kcal/396kJ; Protein 2.2g; Carbohydrate 21.4g, of which sugars 19.2g; Fat 0.4g, of which saturates 0.1g; Cholesterol 0mg; Calcium 39mg; Fibre 2.4g; Sodium 8mg.

**Quince sambal:** (serves 4) Energy 20kcal/85kJ; Protein 0.4g; Carbohydrate 4.8g, of which sugars 4.4g; Fat 0.1g, of which saturates 0g; Cholesterol 0mg; Calcium 10mg; Fibre 0.3g; Sodium 493mg.

**Papaya sambal:** (serves 4) Energy 58kcal/245kJ; Protein 1.1g; Carbohydrate 13.3g, of which sugars 11.2g; Fat 0.3g, of which saturates 0g; Cholesterol 0mg; Calcium 42mg; Fibre 2.6g; Sodium 10mg.

**Armmans pudding:** (Serves 6) Energy 1648kcal/6911kJ; Protein 19.8g; Carbohydrate 214.9g, of which sugars 151.4g; Fat 84.8g, of which saturates 50.5g; Cholesterol 433mg; Calcium 313mg; Fibre 3.5g; Sodium 992mg.

**Melktert:** (serves 8) Energy 302kcal/1262kJ; Protein 8.1g; Carbohydrate 27.3g, of which sugars 12.2g; Fat 17.3g, of which saturates 8.3g; Cholesterol 157mg; Calcium 113mg; Fibre 0g; Sodium 217mg.

**Malva pudding with Van Der Hum sauce:** (serves 6–8) Energy 606kcal/2541kJ; Protein 6.6g; Carbohydrate 78g, of which sugars 54.2g; Fat 30.4g, of which saturates 18.2g; Cholesterol 132mg; Calcium 118mg; Fibre 1.3g; Sodium 470mg.

**Coconut tart:** (serves 6–8) Energy 654kcal/2730kJ; Protein 7.8g; Carbohydrate 56.2g, of which sugars 45.1g; Fat 45.9g, of which saturates 31.4g; Cholesterol 147mg; Calcium 66mg; Fibre 8g; Sodium 296mg.

**Koeksisters:** (makes 12) Energy 195kcal/824kJ; Protein 3.8g; Carbohydrate 39.2g, of which sugars 22.6g; Fat 3.6g, of which saturates 1.7g; Cholesterol 44mg; Calcium 69mg; Fibre 0.9g; Sodium 266mg.

**Amarula nut truffles:** (makes 24) Energy 165kcal/689kJ; Protein 1.8g; Carbohydrate 16.9g, of which sugars 16.7g; Fat 10.3g, of which saturates 5.9g; Cholesterol 40mg; Calcium 14mg; Fibre 0.9g; Sodium 16mg.

**Butternut squash bread:** (2 loaves) Energy 1842kcal/7797kJ; Protein 53.1g; Carbohydrate 341.6g, of which sugars 27.1g; Fat 38.7g, of which saturates 9.6g; Cholesterol 144mg; Calcium 924mg; Fibre 21.9g; Sodium 2143mg.

**Beer bread:** (makes 1 loaf) Energy 1766kcal/7483kJ; Protein 40.6g; Carbohydrate 350.3g, of which sugars 53.6g; Fat 27.3g, of which saturates 4g; Cholesterol 66mg; Calcium 547mg; Fibre 17.1g; Sodium 2032mg.

**Picnic bread and mason jar salad:** (serves 4) Energy 1112kcal/4662kJ; Protein 42g; Carbohydrate 117.5g, of which sugars 11.5g; Fat 56g, of which saturates 18.5g; Cholesterol 247mg; Calcium 675mg; Fibre 10.4g; Sodium 1112mg.

**Western Cape green fig konfyt:** (makes 1kg/2¼lb)Energy 2209kcal/9434kJ; Protein 9.8g; Carbohydrate 575.7g, of which sugars 570g; Fat 1.5g, of which saturates 0.5g; Cholesterol 0mg; Calcium 508mg; Fibre 10g; Sodium 13600mg.

**Quince jam:** (makes 1 litre/1¾ pints/4 cups) Energy 3412kcal/14540kJ; Protein 3g; Carbohydrate 903g, of which sugars 903g; Fat 1g, of which saturates 0g; Cholesterol 0mg; Calcium 220mg; Fibre 0g; Sodium 70mg.

**Apricot jam:** (makes 1.75 litres/3 pints/7½ cups) Energy 679kcal/2828kJ; Protein 32.7g; Carbohydrate 32.2g, of which sugars 2.6g; Fat 47.5g, of which saturates 4.8g; Cholesterol 0mg; Calcium 29mg; Fibre 2g; Sodium 132mg.

**Pineapple and ginger beer with pumpkin pips:** (makes 4 litres/8½ pints/16 cups) Energy 6116kcal/25971kJ; Protein 68.3g; Carbohydrate 1319.9g, of which sugars 1258.3g; Fat 98.8g, of which saturates 15.4g; Cholesterol 0mg; Calcium 776mg; Fibre 10.1g; Sodium 6228mg.

**Rooibos ice tea cocktail:** (serves 2) Energy 184kcal/771kJ; Protein 1.7g; Carbohydrate 24.8g, of which sugars 24.8g; Fat 0.1g, of which saturates 0g; Cholesterol 0mg; Calcium 10mg; Fibre 0.1g; Sodium 33mg.

**Van der Hum-style liqueur:** (makes 800ml/1½ pints/3¼ cups) Energy 2512kcal/10504kJ; Protein 0g; Carbohydrate 195.2g, of which sugars 195.2g; Fat 0g, of which saturates 0g; Cholesterol 0mg; Calcium 0mg; Fibre 0g; Sodium 48mg.

# INDEX

*With thanks to Nicki for her devotion to the project, almighty effort, love, fire lighting instruction and friendship, Oisin and Blaithin for remembering who we were, Alison and Derek Dowey for their big help with matters back home, and Monica and Bill Connolly who did so much to help out with the project.*

# ACKNOWLEDGEMENTS

Special thanks to the good people of South Africa who welcomed us into their homes, farms and hostelries, modelled, held things, posed and were utterly wonderful, especially Charles and Charlene at Natte Valleij Farm; staying in their lovely cottage we were also able to work in the magnificent grounds of the homestead, also meeting friendly staff, like Liam who helped cook the Prego roll. Kelvin and Sandy Quinn for help and fine hospitality. Uncle Frankie and Gladys too. Darren Wygers, for never shirking an opinion and being a good egg. Christien and Handre Durand for all the help, especially Christien for her insight, endless enthusiasm, sourcing, and good humour. Pauline Moses, for her help and insight. Kostas Stavrinos for help with testing and developing the recipes. Matt at Planet of the Grapes. Plush Props at the Biscuit Mill, Cape Town, Craig Siney from Farm Films, and Karoo Moon for lending us the big yellow pot!

Joanne Rippin for keeping us all on track with great humour, for always being on the end of the phone, and Joanna Lorenz for commissioning the project.

Wayne at Skaapwagtersrus on Carpe Diem Farm, a simple but idyllic cottage set in the most peaceful and beautiful part of Klein Karoo near Barrydale. Even if there was no electricity! www.carpediemfarm.co.za

Andrew and Ruth for their warm hospitality at their beautifully styled, spacious accommodation at Gelukkie, Paternoster. www.gelukkie.co.za

Alison and Richard at Leopardstone Hill. A great space to work, relax and enjoy the stunning view of Noordhoek bay. www.leopardstone.co.za

Spier Farm and in Particular Angus McIntosh who has the most amazing farm and delightful livestock. www.farmerangus.co.za

The Butcher Man Cape Town For magnificent meat, top advice and help. www.thebutcherman.co.za

Sage Appliances for food processors www.sageappliances.co.uk and Flock & Herd, London, for help and advice on sausage making www.flockandherd.com

This edition is published by Lorenz Books, an imprint of Anness Publishing Ltd, 108 Great Russell Street, London WC1B 3NA; info@anness.com

www.lorenzbooks.com; www.annesspublishing.com; twitter: @Anness_Books

If you like the images in this book and would like to investigate using them for publishing, promotions or advertising, please visit our website www.practicalpictures.com for more information.

© Anness Publishing Ltd 2015

A CIP catalogue record for this book is available from the British Library.

Publisher: Joanna Lorenz
Project editor: Joanne Rippin
Photography and props styling: Nicki Dowey
Food styling: Fergal Connolly
Additional props styling: Christien Durand
Designer: Jane McKenna

PUBLISHERS' NOTE
Although the advice and information in this book are believed to be accurate and true at the time of going to press, neither the authors nor the publisher can accept any legal responsibility or liability for any errors or omissions that may have been made nor for any inaccuracies nor for any loss, harm or injury that comes about from following instructions or advice in this book.

Thanks to the following agencies for their images:
Alamy, pages 68-69, 80 and 81; Bridgeman Art Library, page 10.

NOTES
Bracketed terms are intended for American readers.
For all recipes, quantities are given in both metric and imperial measures and, where appropriate, in standard cups and spoons. Follow one set of measures, but not a mixture, because they are not interchangeable.

Standard spoon and cup measures are level. 1 tsp = 5ml, 1 tbsp = 15ml, 1 cup = 250ml/8fl oz.

Australian standard tablespoons are 20ml. Australian readers should use 3 tsp in place of 1 tbsp for measuring small quantities.

American pints are 16fl oz/2 cups. American readers should use 20fl oz/2.5 cups in place of 1 pint when measuring liquids.

Electric oven temperatures in this book are for conventional ovens. When using a fan oven, the temperature will probably need to be reduced by about 10–20°C/20–40°F. Since ovens vary, you should check with your manufacturer's instruction book for guidance.

Medium (US large) eggs are used unless otherwise stated.